9/12

Pleas
show

Rene

T

urban village schools

Putting relationships at the heart of secondary school organisation and design

James Wetz

CALOUSTE
GULBENKIAN
FOUNDATION

Published by
Calouste Gulbenkian Foundation
UK Branch
50 Hoxton Square
N1 6PB
+44 (0)20 7012 1400
info@gulbenkian.org.uk
www.gulbenkian.org.uk

ISBN 978 1 903080 11 5

British Library Cataloguing-in-Publication Data
A catalogue record for this book is available from the
British Library

Designed by Pentagram and Helen Swansbourne
Printed by Expression Printers Ltd, IP23 8HH

Distributed by Central Books Ltd,
99 Wallis Road, London E9 5LN
T 0845 458 9911, F 0845 458 9912
orders@centralbooks.com
www.centralbooks.com

CONTENTS

ACKNOWLEDGEMENTS

I would like to thank Andrew Barnett and the Calouste Gulbenkian Foundation for the financial support and encouragement that helped make the writing of this book possible, and in particular to Simon Richey for his belief in this project, and Louisa Hooper who has guided the text to publication with such professionalism. This has been a journey with many supporters and key influences in many places. In Bristol John Savage and John Pontin from the Business Community gave very early support for the idea of developing an Urban Village School; at Channel 4 the Head of Current Affairs Dorothy Byrne gave me the rare opportunity to author and present my arguments in the *Dispatches* series, and Martin Weitz of Focus Productions was a strong ally. In the United States, Linda Nathan at Boston Arts Academy, Peggy Kemp at Fenway High School, and Ann Cook at the Urban Academy have all shared their work and philosophy so very generously, and in Denmark Ketty Matthisson and Tove Ketil Lenger introduced me to the Danish educational models which have been a strong influence in shaping the Urban Village School.

In particular I would like to thank Mary Tasker and Jane Thomas of Human Scale Education; and continuing support from academic colleagues, Ros Sutherland, Kim Etherington, and in particular Elizabeth McNess at Bristol University Graduate School of Education. Thanks also go to Sonia Jackson and Douglas Hooper and colleagues at the Centre for Social Policy at Dartington; Heather Geddes, Robin Balbernie and Lynn Raphael Reed who provided critical commentary at an early stage; and to Alice Ballantine Dykes, who has been a research associate on the project, and to Malcolm Hughes at the University of the West of England for his invaluable research advice. In addition I am highly grateful to Peter Clegg, Andy Theobald, Vanessa Warnes and Kinga Szabo at the architectural studios of Feilden Clegg Bradley in Bath who gave so much to this project; and to Max Hammeindorf, Jacob Kestner, Shira Rubin and Bruno Reddy of Teach First who are pioneering new approaches and whose comments have influenced the text.

Finally I would like to thank my wife Diana, who with her expertise and advice as a therapist in Child and Adolescent Mental Health has been supportive of my endeavours and who is also my constant friend and critic.

James Wetz

FOREWORD

The Foundation has a reputation for innovation and for backing those with the ideas and idealism to help effect its purpose – enriching and connecting the experiences of individuals to secure lasting and beneficial change. A key aim in its work is to assist individuals, especially the vulnerable, to fulfil their potential in society, and the successful education of young people lies at the heart of this aim. Convinced by growing evidence that students learn best in small-scale settings, for the past three years the Foundation has been supporting the introduction of human scale practices into selected secondary schools and evaluating the impact.

It was in this context that we read *Holding Children in Mind Over Time* (2006), a report by James Wetz, formerly a headteacher in Bristol of many years experience. The report identified the characteristics of a cohort of pupils who had recently left Bristol's mainstream secondary schools aged 16 without any formal qualifications. It then considered how secondary schools, both in Bristol and, by implication, beyond, could be so designed and organised as to respond better to the educational and emotional needs of all pupils, in particular the less resilient. A critical finding of the report was that their current design and organisation (including the size of school, curriculum, assessment and teacher pupil relationships) limited schools' capacity to meet the depth of pupils' emotional and social needs. It concluded with a key recommendation, namely that a feasibility study should be conducted that proposed an alternative model for the state sector – for *all* pupils and not simply the less resilient – and that explored its design and organisation as well as cost implications. These ideas resonated with the Foundation's commitment to human scale education and made James Wetz's proposed feasibility study a natural candidate for our support.

The result is the present book. The model it proposes, or the Urban Village School of the title, is shaped by a number of influences: the testimonies of disaffected young people interviewed by the author, examples of human scale education from other countries and, not least, the psychological and developmental factors that make for a successful childhood. At the heart of the model is the importance of relationships in schools and central to the conduct of good relationships is a human scale environment where the large and impersonal is replaced by the small and more intimate.

This emphasis on the small scale may run the risk of appearing naïve in the present educational climate. Is it reasonable, it might be objected, to propose the creation of small state secondary schools where national policy favours the opening of ever greater numbers of large Academies? Is it cost effective? Is it even consistent with the Government's guidelines for new school buildings? The author acknowledges that these are among the most common questions put to him when he speaks publicly and in the book he is at pains to answer them.

It is encouraging to report that the notion of Urban Village Schools has attracted a considerable amount of attention, bolstered by the transmission on Channel 4 in February 2008 of 'The Children Left Behind', a *Dispatches* programme on the subject. Partly as a result of this, the author has been engaged by local authorities, Academy leaders, parent and community groups and others to help them translate some of the ideas that underpin the notion of an Urban Village School into practice.

As the author emphasises, this model is not intended to be prescriptive but rather 'an illustration of how we might rethink the organisation and design of our secondary schools by exploiting the advantages of human scale'. The Government's Building Schools for the Future programme, as well as the greater freedom afforded parents, community groups and others to open new schools, makes this an especially propitious time for such 'rethinking'. We hope this book plays its part in encouraging the development of an education system that enables all young people to fulfil their potential and contribute to our society.

Andrew Barnett
Director
Calouste Gulbenkian Foundation UK Branch

INTRODUCTION

Over 20,000 young people each year give up on going to school by the age of 14, over 35,000 leave with no GCSE qualifications at all, and more than 140,000 leave with no GCSEs above Grade D.[1] Despite the very best efforts of our teachers and our education system, there is a widening gap between the young people who are achieving in our schools and the growing disaffection, alienation and anger of a significant and increasing underclass who leave with few qualifications, little chance of worthwhile employment, and no stake in our society.

In an earlier report, *Holding Children in Mind over Time*, I broached the question: how fit for purpose is the design and organisation of our secondary schools?[2] In *Urban Village Schools* I seek to address this issue. Drawing on three sources of information: the voices of disaffected young people, international examples of human scale educational practice, and the psychological and developmental factors that make for a successful childhood, I provide principles for rethinking the way we design and organise our secondary schools, and use these to formulate a new model of schooling for our inner city communities. I develop the model of an 'Urban Village School' as a learning *community*, which puts relationships at the heart of its organisation and design, and include an architect's view of what such a school could look like in practice.

Chapter One gives an overview of the challenges facing our schools, our teachers, and our young people. Why have so many young people become disengaged from our educational provision at secondary school level? Is there a 'crisis of childhood' in the UK? Are the problems we face caused by young people themselves or by adult society, which has adopted a discourse of control rather than care in its approach to young people? Are teachers and schools equipped to cope successfully with challenging behaviour? Drawing on recent commentators and reports, including the 2007 UNICEF report on child wellbeing, the Good Childhood Inquiry, the Joseph Rowntree report, *Tackling Low Educational Achievement*, and *Holding Children in Mind over Time*, I identify some key factors that undermine the experience of secondary school for both pupils and teachers.[3] Is the government's Building School's for the Future (BSF) programme addressing these issues or do we need to look at other initiatives to inform the organisation and design of our secondary schools?

Chapter Two draws on the insights and perceptions of four disaffected young people who were unable to engage positively in secondary schooling. Kirsten, Harry, Devlin and Jacky are part of the 10 per cent of young people who left Bristol's mainstream secondary schools in 2004 without a single GCSE qualification, although, as with 40 per cent of such young people, they had achieved Level 4 or above in mathematics, science or English at Key Stage 2, at the end of their primary schooling.[4]

They tell their stories of school and family life in the hope that this might influence educational leaders and policy makers to improve the schooling experience of young people in the future. Common themes emerge: significant disruption and discontinuity within family life; a sense of isolation at home and school; a sharp contrast between their experiences at primary and secondary school; a lack of safe, reliable and consistent adult support in secondary school; and a lack of resilience to manage large secondary school settings, leading to self-exclusion often from as early as 14.

Chapter Three considers what lessons can be learned from abroad, in particular from the small school movement in the USA and the educational system in Denmark. These are 'human scale' approaches, which put relationships at the heart of school organisation and design. Taught a flexible, inter-disciplinary curriculum in smaller classes, by fewer teachers, pupils are well known by staff and challenged to learn and behave to the highest standards. The staff collaborates as a professional community, thinking, planning and reflecting on its work, and provides young people with a constructive experience of living in community, which they can take into their adult lives. Recent evaluation of small schools in Boston (the Boston Pilot Schools) showed improved outcomes in attendance, exclusion rates, academic achievement and graduation rates compared to other Boston schools, although the Pilot Schools have not proved more expensive to run.[5]

Chapter Four explores the factors that make for a successful childhood and the implications these have for the design and organisation of secondary schools. Theoretical models of 'attachment' suggest that children need a reliable 'attachment figure' and a 'secure base in relationships' in order to be able to trust, contain anxiety, regulate emotions and be open to learning. I argue that secondary schools must offer a secure base and reliable attachment figures who understand that challenging behaviour is a communication about need, if all young people are to flourish at school. I consider what we can learn from the policy and practice in therapeutic educational settings, which work with some our most troubled and distressed young people, and the implications for teacher training, continuing professional development and professional supervision of teachers, if the lessons of attachment theory are to be applied in secondary schools.

Chapter Five proposes one model for an 'Urban Village School' developed from the principles we have learned from the stories of disaffected young people, international examples of human scale education, and the psychological and developmental factors that make for a successful childhood. These principles are applied to create a research and learning community of 375 11–16 year olds, where staff teach no more than 75 pupils a week, and relationships are placed at the heart of the school's organisation and design. The timetable is flexible, organised around Learning, Assessment and Community Programmes, and the teaching cross-curricular. Underpinning the Urban Village School is a theoretical framework based in attachment theory and there is an emphasis on staff training and development. The Urban Village School is not a prescriptive model but rather an illustration of how we might rethink the organisation and design of our secondary schools by exploiting the advantages of human scale. The model also challenges the existing orthodoxy of large school communities and their current rebuilding as huge academies.

Chapter Six provides plans and visualisations of an Urban Village School developed by award-winning architects, Feilden Clegg Bradley. The first conceptual drawings illustrate how the theoretical framework shapes the model, and the plans, sections and detail of the design demonstrate how government guidelines for school design and organisation (BB98) can accommodate the urban village concept. I describe how the architects developed the 'internal intellectual architecture' of the school and then we take a 'virtual walk' through it.

But does it really matter if the secondary education system fails some of our young people? During the final preparations for the publication of *Urban Village Schools*, a newspaper headline announced: 'One in six long-term young jobless "dead within ten years"'.[6] The article suggests that there has been a surge in the number of 'NEETs', British youngsters aged 16 to 24 who are not in education, employment or training. There are now 935,000 young people in this position – almost 16 per cent of this age group. In one British city a study, quoted by Jon Coles the Government's Director General of Schools, found that:

> 'Those who had been outside the system for a long time, whether because they were permanently excluded or simply because they had dropped out at the end of compulsory schooling and had not got into anything else, 15 per cent of those young people of ten years ago were dead by the time the research was done. ... For those of us who sometimes console ourselves with the thought that education is not a matter of life and death, actually for the most vulnerable children and young people in our society it really is.'

CHAPTER ONE
The challenges facing our young people, teachers and schools

'One of the biggest problems facing British schools is the gap between rich and poor, and the enormous disparity in children's home backgrounds and the social and cultural capital they bring to the educational table.'

M. Benn and F. Millar, *A Comprehensive Future* (2006)[7]

After more than 30 years working in state education, 16 of these as a headteacher of two large secondary schools, I have been left reflecting deeply on the reasons why some young people find it too difficult to learn in our schools. What is it about school design and organisation that makes it so hard for these young people, despite all our efforts and imagination, to make the most of their schooling? This book sets out to explore and address this question.

At the heart of my concern is the widening gap between the very many young people who are achieving in our schools and the growing disaffection, alienation and anger of a significant and increasing underclass who are not, who leave school with few if any qualifications, with hardly any chance of employment or any interest in training, and with little stake in mainstream society.

Where schools have a significant number of these young people, they can create an overwhelming challenge despite all reasonable efforts in current settings to help them. The threat that they pose causes even the most liberal school system to resort to sanctions which further alienates these young people, creating considerable custodial and social costs down the line. The way we respond to the 'disaffected and difficult to engage young' is critical for them as individuals, for the success of our school system as a whole and for the health of our society. But first we need to understand why they are so disaffected and so difficult to engage and use this understanding to inform the organisation and design of our schools.

The family and the school are the two main social institutions which support young people on a 'safe journey' from childhood to young adulthood. If the family is distressed and unable to provide the love, care, guidance and consistent parenting that young people need, then the school becomes an even more important influence. Increasingly, schools must be prepared to act as a 'corporate parent' and be designed and organised to fulfil wider social responsibilities. I believe that the model which best meets these responsibilities and the needs of our disaffected young people is for a much smaller secondary school than is currently usual in the state sector. These smaller schools are 'human scale' and founded on the importance of building, maintaining and developing close, supportive and important relationships. I call them 'Urban Village Schools'.

Urban Village Schooling is an approach which is in the interests not only of those currently marginalised by our school system, but of all young people. It is a model that has been developed with our inner cities in mind, hence the name, but is applicable in any setting. It seeks to prevent the institutional exclusion of all young people who find it difficult to engage with our current system.

A crisis of childhood and adolescence in the UK

With the abundance of research data and reports on British teenagers emerging in recent years, it is difficult to avoid the question: is there a 'crisis of childhood' in the UK? Kevin Haines and Mark Drakeford make a more fundamental assertion at the beginning of their book, *Young People and Youth Justice*, namely that 'our society does not like young people.'[8] Barry Goldson, Senior Lecturer in Sociology at the University of Liverpool, reports a burgeoning sense of adult anxiety in relation to the young, of children apparently beyond the law, of a new moral panic which increasingly sees the child as a danger.[9] In a contribution to *Children and Contemporary Society* he writes:

> 'Institutional demonization rests upon spurious domain assumptions. Individual agency is profiled, personal responsibility is piously ascribed, and structural context is just as emphatically denied ... The Bulger trial was not an aberration. Holding children (as young as ten years, and in certain cases younger) to be as responsible as adults is now endemic through the "justice" process in England and Wales ... expanded forms of child incarceration, longer sentences, "fast track" punishment, pervasive "toughness" ... all add up to institutionalised demonization and criminalisation.'[10]

This is obviously not a new anxiety. Over ten years ago Wendy Stainton Rogers, Professor of Health Psychology at the Open University, wrote:

'Now children have become dangerous to us ... we have become scared of their sexual precocity and their violent instincts, and we have made them into society's scapegoats ... our response is to adopt a discourse of control rather than a discourse of welfare.'[11]

A discourse of control and contract, not welfare

Some would argue that what Rogers terms the 'discourse of control' creates unhappy young people. In a 2008 article in the *New Statesman*, journalist and commentator Suzanne Moore asks: 'Why are our young people so unhappy?' and answers: 'Because we have become a society that fears, demonises and silences them. The fault is ours, not theirs.'[12] The article is a powerful and angry polemic expressing the frustration of young people. Moore argues that:

'Overtesting our children has not made them cleverer; criminalising them has not made them behave better ... countries that are doing better than us do so because therapeutic and family interventions are not only more effective than punishment but also cheaper.'[13]

Another recent contributor to this debate is psychotherapist and trainer Rachel Wingfield, who writes:

'It deeply concerns me that, so many years after the birth of attachment theory, an understanding of the impacts of separation and loss and trauma are still missing from any understanding of disaffected or so called anti-social behaviour in our young people.'[14]

Wingfield notes how John Bowlby, the British psychologist who originally developed the theory of attachment, highlighted our basic need for secure relationships and for society to provide a culture of stability, inclusion and belonging for its children.[15] Wingfield argues that where stability, inclusion and belonging are absent we see an increase in young people being involved in gangs and cults. A recent front-page headline in *The Guardian* reminds us of the stark reality of the consequences of poor attachments for our young people: 'Gangs are getting younger and more violent, Met chief warns.'[16] Commentators such as the sociologist Professor Bill Jordan (University of Exeter) also identify a discourse of control in our approach to children, which rests on the assumption that inherently children lack control and hence need to be regulated.[17] This discourse shapes education policy by obliging children to be educated and imposing excessive regulation over the manner and content. In contrast, a discourse of welfare would be based on the assumption that children are entitled to a 'good childhood' and that they need support and protection. Towards the end of his life, Bowlby complained that the world's richest countries had ignored the fact that 'caring for children' was an 'indispensable social role' and that we 'had created a topsy turvy world' in which pursuit of wealth had replaced the need for relationships.[18]

As Professor Wendy Stainton Rogers says:

> 'If we are to work toward achieving a better quality of life for children ... we need the vision to imagine what better childhoods might be and a determination to achieve the conditions that will make those better childhoods possible.'[19]

In *Social Values in Policies for Children*, Jordan explains how the current Labour administration has spelled out what (arguably) remained implicit under previous Conservative governments, that 'contract has replaced culture as the regulatory principle' and now in the fields of child care and youth justice 'contracts have become the instruments of choice ... as a way to modify behaviour and induce change.' In other words:

> 'The relationship between the public official and the individual child is defined as a contractual one ... and the problem to be addressed is often stated in terms of culture (drug culture, gun culture, benefits culture).'[20]

Jordan concludes his paper by saying that:

> 'If the malaise of British childhood – obesity, lack of exercise, insecurity, bullying, risky behaviour as well as deprivation and disability – are to be addressed as aspects of the same set of problems, then more attention has to be directed at the collective infrastructure of ideas, feelings, relationships, and systems of membership in which children are growing up.'

The British journalist Madeleine Bunting makes a similar plea:

> 'It's a pathology of individual entitlement – what's crumbling is the civility that is essential to our wellbeing, to trust and to the conviviality of our lives. We have failed to invest the resources, both material and cultural, in the places where we interact with strangers.'[21]

The UNICEF report on child wellbeing

The 2007 UNICEF report, *Child poverty in perspective*, described UK children as some of the least nurtured in the developed world.[22]

The report sought to assess 'whether children feel loved, cherished, special and supported, within the family and community, and whether the family and community are being supported in this task by public policy and resources'. The findings showed that in the UK:

- child poverty had doubled since 1979;
- 16 per cent of children were living in homes earning less than half the national wage; and
- only 43 per cent of children rated their peers as kind and helpful.

Responses to the report were uncompromising. The Children's Commissioner for England, Sir Al Aynsley-Green said:

> 'We are turning out a generation of young people who are unhappy, unhealthy, engaging in risky behaviour, who have poor relationships with their family and their peers, who have low expectations and don't feel safe'.[23]

Collette Marshall, the UK Director of Save the Children, used the word 'shameful' to describe the fact that the UK was at the bottom of the Child Well-Being table.[24] Jonathan Bradshaw, Professor of Social Policy at the University of York and one of the report's authors, expressed the view that at the heart of the problem 'is a society which is very unequal, with high levels of poverty' and that this influences what 'children think about themselves and their lives'.[25]

The question of the impact of inequality on societies has also been highlighted by Richard Wilkinson and Kate Pickett, academic epidemiologists at the Universities of Nottingham and York respectively, who argue convincingly that the quality of social relations is built on material foundations: 'The scale of income difference has a powerful effect on the way we relate to each other.' They are convinced that 'the quality of social relations deteriorates in less equal societies' and that 'both the broken society and the broken economy resulted from the growth of inequality.'[26]

In addition, I would suggest that 'income difference' is also strongly related to the scale of 'attachment deficit' that children experience in families that are affected by levels of poverty.

Wilkinson and Picket also make the point that 'social anxiety is on the increase' and argue that it is related to the break-up of settled communities:

'People's sense of identity used to be embedded in the community to which they belonged, in people's real knowledge of each other, but now it is cast adrift in the anonymity of mass society … familiar faces have been replaced by a constant flux of strangers.'[27]

Nowhere is this more apparent that in large secondary schools:

'While [adolescents'] sense of themselves is most uncertain – they have to cope in schools of a thousand and more of their peers. It is hardly surprising that peer pressure becomes such a powerful force in their lives, and that so many are dissatisfied with what they look like, or succumb to depression and self harm.'[28]

The Good Childhood Inquiry

In 2006, The Children's Society launched The Good Childhood Inquiry. The resulting report, *A Good Childhood: Searching for values in a competitive age*, published in 2009, also emphasises the impact of social inequality on educational outcomes in the UK. It reports a school system blighted by social inequality and by the widening gap between those who are achieving well in our secondary schools and those who are not, and quotes figures for 2006 of only 28 per cent of children in the most deprived quarter of schools gaining five or more GCSE passes at A*–C compared to 68 per cent of children in the least deprived quarter of schools.[29]

The report found that, after the USA, the UK is the most unequal of the rich countries. In Britain 22 per cent of children are poor (defined as living below 60 per cent of typical income) compared to 8 per cent in Sweden and 10 per cent in Denmark. 30 years ago the figure for the UK was only 13 per cent.

Further The Good Childhood Inquiry more found that, in a survey on values and discipline in our schools, 29 per cent of 11–14 year olds in metropolitan areas said that every day other pupils tried to disrupt their learning; 43 per cent said that other pupils were 'always' or 'often' so noisy that they found it difficult to work. The report comments that 'disorder on this scale is highly disturbing.'

On mental health it noted that 10 per cent of all 5–16 year olds now have clinically significant mental health difficulties – ranging from anxiety, depression, over activity, inattentiveness (ADHD), and anorexia, through to conduct disorders such as uncontrollable and destructive behaviour. The report highlights that in nearly every survey the proportion of children with behavioural problems is at least 50 per cent higher in families with single parents or step-parents than in families where both parents are still together. By the age of 16, a third of British children are living apart from their biological father, and children whose parents separate are 50 per cent more likely, says the report, to fail at school, and to suffer behavioural difficulties, anxiety or depression.

The report adds that 90 per cent of adolescents convicted of crime had shown conduct disorder in childhood. By the time they are 28 years old a young person with conduct disorder on average costs the taxpayer £70,000 in crime, social care and remedial costs compared to £7,000 for a child without such problems. Teenage pregnancies are higher in the UK than anywhere in Western Europe at 27 per 1,000 compared to only 5 per 1,000 in the Netherlands.

The levels and effects of abuse on children

In 2008 *The Lancet* published a series of papers in collaboration with the Royal College of Paediatrics and Child Health detailing the level of maltreatment of children, which identified that in the UK one in ten children suffers physical, sexual and/or emotional abuse or neglect.[30]

In the UK, the report found that:

- 10 per cent of children suffered emotional abuse every year (defined as persistently being made to feel worthless, unwanted or scared);
- more than 15 per cent suffered neglect (defined as the failure of their parents or carers to meet a child's basic emotional or physical needs or ensure their safety); and
- 5–10 per cent of girls and 1–5 per cent of boys had been subjected to penetrative sex, usually by a family friend or relative.

Maltreated children perform poorly in our schools, and are at risk of becoming violent and involved in crime. They are more likely to join gangs, turn to alcohol, drugs and prostitution, suffer depression and commit suicide. Yet whilst teachers are often best placed to spot abuse, they are not resourced to support such children, have little access to social workers in order to design appropriate interventions, and little training on the impact of abuse on those they teach or how to respond to this.

The Rowntree Report

The Joseph Rowntree report, *Tackling Low Educational Achievement*, published in June 2007, highlighted the tens of thousands of pupils in

England who leave school aged 16 without a single GCSE or very limited qualifications.[31] The report set out factors associated with low achievement. Nearly half of all low achievers are white British males; boys outnumber girls by three to two; low achievement is linked to eligibility to free school meals; poor reading and writing at primary schools are linked with later low achievement; low achievers are commonly found in poor urban areas; those who leave schools with no passes at all number 5 per cent and those with no pass better than D make up 25 per cent of school leavers in the state system. These students are likely to be badly placed for the job market, and in general inadequately prepared for participation in society. Many of them are at risk of unemployment or even falling into low-level criminal activity.

What is clear from the Rowntree report research data is a consensus about what the issues are:

- a persistent minority of schools continue to underperform;
- progress in literacy and numeracy at 11 seems hard to raise;
- too many young people reach 16 with a lack of basic skills and leave school with no formal qualifications;
- the performance of boys is weaker than that of girls;
- parents' socio-economic status still affects GCSE performance; and
- the gaps between those who are achieving in our schools and those who are not is widening.

The report's assessment of educational achievement in the UK links closely to the effects of such poor performance on the increasing numbers of young people who are leaving our schools with few qualifications. The Office for National Statistics details that between 1997 and 2007 the numbers of young people aged between 15 and 24 who are not in education, on a training scheme or in employment, has risen by 15 per cent to 2.4 million. Specifically the rise in 16 and 17 years olds who are not in education, training or employment, has increased over the same period by 30 per cent. When these numbers are turned into descriptions – the narratives of young people's experiences – then the hurt and loss that this represents for those concerned is considerable.

A high number of school exclusions in the UK

Drawing on other recent studies, *Tackling Low Educational Achievement* also highlights how exclusions are a characteristic of school under-performance.[32] The report suggests that data available in 2007 showed that 12 young people in every 10,000 are permanently excluded from mainstream schools in England, 80 per cent of these from secondary schools. Of these, young people with special educational needs are over-represented at the rate of 8:1; the ratio of boys to girls being excluded is 4:1; and one in every 250 of 13–14 year olds is excluded before they get to start their GCSE programme. The highest rates of exclusion are amongst black boys, with black girls being three times more likely to be excluded than white girls, and with 'looked-after children' being significantly over-represented.

Perhaps the most worrying development in recent years is the increase in fixed period exclusions, which according to DCSF statistics had reached over 360,000 a year in secondary schools in 2007 and 45,700 in primary schools. Of these suspensions nearly 350 a day are for violence against other pupils, prompting deep concern about the health and welfare of our young people.[33] We are clearly not designing educational provision that meets the needs of many of our young people, and with which they can positively engage.

The implications of exclusion

So what happens when children are unable to engage with their schooling in a positive way? It is certainly impacting on the youth justice system. Nearly 100,000 young people aged 10–17 enter the youth justice system in the UK every year and the government is pledged to reduce this by 20 per cent by 2020.[34] In a Home Office report issued in April 2009 86 per cent of young men and 79 per cent of young women aged 15–18 in young offender institutions had been excluded from school. Around a third were under 14 when they last attended school.[35]

The Prison Reform Trust's Bromley Briefings prison fact file, June 2009, sets out key data on the prosecution of young people, which makes for uncomfortable reading. It shows that crime rates are falling throughout Britain yet the number of children being prosecuted keeps rising. 93,730 young people were first-time entrants into the Youth Justice System in 2006–7. Judges and magistrates are jailing young offenders at an unprecedented rate. Ministry of Justice figures obtained in parliamentary questions showed that there were 5,165 young people aged 15–17 who entered prison in 2008. The number of girls aged 10–17 sentenced to custody at magistrates' courts increased 181 per cent between 1996 and 2006. The data also shows that 71 per cent of children in custody were involved with or in the care of social services before entering custody. 40 per cent of children in custody have previously been homeless and have suffered severe social exclusion and 75 per cent of those released in 2007 re-offended within a year.[36]

In an interview for the *Dispatches* programme 'The Children Left Behind', I asked Rod Morgan, former Chairman of the Youth Justice Board, about the impact of so many young people failing to engage with schooling as it is currently designed and organised. His answer was a direct challenge to the educational system:

> 'The consequences of young people not engaging in education, either not going, or being formally excluded, is that they are much more likely to get into trouble with the police and to engage in offending behaviour and then come before the courts. The truth is that the answers have more to do with our educational system than anything that can be achieved in the youth courts.'[37]

Holding Children in Mind over Time

In 2006 I published a regional report, *Holding Children in Mind over Time*, based on a study of the 10 per cent of young people leaving Bristol's schools in 2004 without any GCSE qualifications. It called for a radical rethink about the way we organise and design our schools to allow those most at risk of under achieving to be more successful. The report suggested that:

> 'A significant number of the disaffected young might well be those who have lacked affection and are acting out a remembered hurt of separation, loss, neglect, abuse, or less than secure attachment, which schools as they are currently designed and organised have neither the expertise or resource to recognise and attend to.'[38]

It is important to stress that some young people may disengage from school out of boredom, refusing to 'play an educational game' they find increasingly dull or irrelevant or that makes them feel inadequate. For some, their disruptive behaviour may be a reflection of disrupted lives over which they have little control. For others, a rejection of what secondary schools offer may be based in self-confidence – they will find their own route to adulthood outside of the school setting – and demonstrates not a lack of resilience but a strong capacity for self-determination.

However, whether the issues are caused by disaffection, disengagement or determination, the Bristol research highlighted a particular concern: 40 per cent of those who left the city's maintained secondary schools without a single GCSE qualification had achieved average or above average results in English, mathematics or science at primary school (i.e. Level 4 or above at Key Stage 2). These students might reasonably have expected to achieve five good GCSEs, secure places in Post 16 courses and gain access to further or higher education.

Holding Children in Mind over Time also revealed that those who left the school system with no GCSE qualifications were young people who had had to manage complex emotional and social changes in their lives. For example, they had:

- experienced a sense of isolation both at home and at school;
- undergone many changes in family and school settings between the ages of five and 16;
- experienced significant early loss and separation, particularly from absent fathers; and/or
- felt that the reliability, care, safety and consistency that they had enjoyed at primary school were not available to them at secondary school.

As a result, many had effectively excluded themselves from learning in school before they had reached the age of 14. It would seem that disadvantaged pupils pay 'the highest price' in our large secondary schools. They arrive needing the most academic enrichments and most adult advocacy, and routinely they leave having received the least.

Holding Children in Mind over Time argued that, if the stories of those it featured are representative of the wider group of young people who leave school with few if any qualifications, then there is a compelling case for reconsidering the design and organisation of our secondary schools so that these less resilient young people can stay safe and well, achieve qualifications and enjoy their learning.

The impact on teachers

Whilst I have focused on the position of young people, there is rising concern for the emotional health and wellbeing of our teachers. If *The Observer* Focus report in 2008 on 'Schools under strain' reflects the current position, then the statistics on teacher stress should be ringing alarm bells.[39] The report quotes a range of research. A YouGov survey in 2007 found that half of all teachers had thought about quitting because of stress, and research by the Teacher Support Network in the same year found that over 70 per cent of Scottish teachers felt their job was ruining their health. The numbers of teachers retiring early has doubled in the last ten years – in 2008 10,270 left the profession early compared with 5,580 in 1998.

What is clear from all these reports is the consistency of concern about the welfare of our children and teachers. They underline a compelling need for a radical and systemic change to the design and organisation of our schools which draws on relevant intelligence and data in order to begin to address concerns about both our young people and the teachers charged with their care and education.

Building Schools for the Future: a key response from the Government

The Government is investing unprecedented sums of money in our schooling system through the Building Schools for the Future (BSF) programme. It has set out a plan that over the next 15 years most secondary schools in England will be transformed through a nation-wide programme of refurbishment, adaptations and new buildings. This programme is the largest single capital investment programme in schools in 50 years and the intention is to rebuild or renew all of England's state secondary schools, where there is a need, to create buildings that:

- drive reform of the secondary system and improvements in educational standards;
- are good places for teachers to teach and pupils to learn, supported by ICT;
- are used by the community;
- are well designed, built on time and at a reasonable cost to the taxpayer, and are properly maintained over their lives.[40]

The BSF programme is being developed and modified as it moves forward and has the crucial aim of going beyond the renewal of buildings to support more fundamental educational reform. The most significant emphases are on building schools which give communities a sense of identity, creating consistency of provision, paying attention to issues of conservation in buildings of architectural or historic interest, enabling regeneration within communities, securing the involvement of all stakeholders in the best design solutions, and ensuring sustainability.

However, it is difficult to find anywhere in the Government's documentation for this massive capital investment programme a clear link between school design, school organisation, and addressing the needs of the growing number of young people who are disengaged from the educational process.

My argument is that the current design and organisation of our secondary schools is to a great extent institutionally excluding many young people and that the BSF programme may make matters worse not better. The question is: how might we create the settings where all our young people can engage positively in learning and grow up into young adults with a stake in mainstream society, looking back on their schooling with affection and a sense of pride and achievement?

I believe that we must look to different kinds of intelligence to help us address the issues we face in relation to so many of our young people. What do young people think, particularly those who have been disengaged and failed to achieve their academic potential? We will hear their voices – often marginalised at best and usually ignored – in the next chapter.

Summary

- *Urban Village Schools* explores the reasons why some young people find it too difficult to learn in our secondary schools and seeks to address this in the interests of all young people, the school system as a whole and the health of our society.
- There is a widening gap between those who are achieving in our schools, and the growing disaffection, anger and alienation of a significant and increasing underclass who leave with few qualifications and little stake in civil society.
- Is there a 'crisis of childhood' in the UK? Increasingly we see young people as a source of disruption and threat, with little understanding that disaffected or 'anti-social' behaviour may be the result of separation, trauma and loss.
- We have taken up a discourse of control, not welfare, in our approach to children's behaviour, which we seek to 'regulate' through contracts rather than nurture through relationships.
- In 2007, the UNICEF report on child poverty described UK children as some of the least nurtured in the developed world. Our society is 'very unequal, with high levels of poverty' and such inequality impacts on wellbeing and educational attainment.
- Recent reports from The Children's Society (*A Good Childhood*, 2009), the Joseph Rowntree Foundation (*Tackling Low Educational Achievement*, 2007) and in *The Lancet* ('On child maltreatment in high-income countries', 2008) have all highlighted the problems faced by our young people in what has been called by some 'a broken society'. By the age of 16 one third of all British children live apart from their biological father.

- The UK has a high number of school exclusions and the consequences are very often negative; over 80 per cent of boys in young
offender institutions have been excluded from school.
- In 2006, the report *Holding Children in Mind over Time* revealed
that 40 per cent of the young people in Bristol leaving school in
2004 without any GCSE qualifications had achieved average or
above average results in English, mathematics or science at primary
school. These were young people who had to manage complex
emotional and social changes in their lives; the organisation and
design of their secondary schools had failed to support their needs.
- There is rising concern for the emotional health and wellbeing of
our teachers. The number of teachers retiring early has doubled in
the last ten years.
- Will the government's Building Schools for the Future programme
address these issues or do we need to look at other sources of
intelligence to inform the organisation and design of secondary
schools?

CHAPTER TWO

Learning from the voices of 'disaffected and difficult to engage' young people

> 'The multiple hurts endured by many participants, adult and child, in the drama of school failure, call out to be healed.'
>
> L. Raphael Reed *et al, Young Participation in Higher Education* (2007)[41]

Here Kirsten and Harry, Jackie and Devlin share their stories of family and school life. They are just four of the young people who agreed to share their stories with me in the hope that they might be able to influence policy makers to think again about the educational offer that is currently available to young people.

Kirsten's story

I enjoyed primary school. I loved working and doing good at school and I had top marks and stuff. And I liked all the teachers there as well, it was a good school. We had one teacher who taught us all the lessons and our class was really close and we were really close to our teacher. This helped and it made me want to work for her even more. We used to have competitions to see who could do the most work and stuff. I wrote 20-page stories when I was at primary school. Our teacher's name was Mrs Ford and she was very nice. She wasn't unfair. She treated us like adults even though we were kids. She wasn't like a teacher. She seemed more like an auntie or something. It was like being in your own little family kind of thing.

When I went up to secondary school, it was all different. I sort of managed Year 7. I wasn't good but I wasn't naughty, just like chatting in lessons and stuff, but I did my work and I was in all the top classes. It was boring mostly. But then I started bunking off a bit and towards the end of Year 8 it got worse and then in Year 9 I'd only go in once every couple of weeks and then I just stopped going in the end.

By Year 8 I got in with all the troublemakers and you just start thinking trouble. I was horrible. I used to beat people up and had this attitude. I thought it was good to be doing the things I was doing. I thought it was good to mess with the teachers. I just thought I was big and bad.

I had a problem with authority. They'd try and say, I'm the adult and you're the child, and say shut up, and you will do this, and don't talk. The teachers would swear and bully and shout in your face. I couldn't take this and at the end of Year 8 I sort of stopped going. I know I was only about 12 years old but I was independent. I thought, I know what I'm doing, that's just how I am. It's because my mum had a drugs problem and so ever since I was young I've had to deal with things on my own.

I just had to get on with things. I have always had to, not fully, but from the age of eight I'd say my mum would only cook now and then but not all the time. I had to wake myself up, get up, do my own breakfast. They'd still be in bed till like half past four in the afternoon, and then they'd get up, smoke their joints, go out earning, come back, score their drugs, smoke and then go back to sleep. But I got myself to primary school because I enjoyed it there.

I'm an only child. We were not a close family. I'm not close to my mum now – yes I love my mum but I'm not close to her like how you see other mums and daughters who talk together and do things together or their mum's interested in their lives. I think that's why I enjoyed primary school so much. It was like your own little family. My step-dad he's up the jail now, he's been up the jail for two years. I don't know my real dad. I sometimes think that I'd like to find about him but then I don't, 'cos I don't know if he wants to know me. If he had wanted to know me then he would have been in touch by now.

I moved out when I was 13. No, it was just before my 13th birthday. I moved out first to my friend's house. She was in her twenties. When I first moved out I was getting myself into trouble. But I helped with my friend's little girl and we'd take trips to see her partner who was in jail in Exeter. I was 13 and she was 22, she was more of a friend than a mother. I've always been with older people.

Reflections

Looking back on all this I don't feel strongly or anything. If I'd had better parents then I'd have been shown a better way and if I'd been to a different school then it would have been different. That's it really. You can't just blame the school though, there were a number of things wrong. But I am sad about all this in a way. I wish I never, I wish I never left school, I wish that I'd never left and that I would have got back in. But then you just end up getting yourself into so much trouble, and then you just can't.

Kirsten achieved Level 4 grades in English, mathematics and science at Key Stage 2 at the end of her primary schooling. She did not sit any Key Stage 3 tests or any GCSE examinations at secondary school.

Harry's story

I changed primary schools at the age of seven. The first primary school I absolutely hated, I think the headteacher had it in for me. There were times which were difficult and stressful. But the second primary school I really liked. It was one of the best schools I've been to. There was more hands on and the teachers helped you, and there were classroom assistants so you did not have to wait for ages to get help. I also got on better with the other kids. I cannot remember the names of the teachers from my first primary school but I can remember them from the second. There was Miss Green who was really nice, she made me feel really welcome and when I arrived she asked this boy Matty to show me round the whole school. I could probably have worked harder but I was happy there, and I did my fair share and came away with quite good grades.

My sister and I had quite a hard time growing up, we only had our mum and money was always really tight. I was just three months old when my dad left and he'd been in and out of prison. We moved primary schools when my mum moved house to be with her boyfriend and they have two small children now. When my mum was pregnant with the second child they had arguments. He ended up hitting mum so he got kicked out when I was in Year 8 at secondary school. I liked him in a way, he was a sort of dad but he was never like a real dad – if I'd ring him and say can you pick me up, he'd be like, no walk home sort of thing.

The secondary school was quite close to the primary school and the majority of kids went there together, which was nice as we had friends and could be together at breaktime and lunchtime. At first I was happy there and successful at my work. I was always in the top sets and I may have bunked off a lesson or two but nothing serious. Then in Year 8, I got into a little trouble just messing around and being cheeky to the teachers. It was not so much that I did not respect the teachers, more that I wanted to impress my mates and obviously when you are that age you think it is funny.

I was in the top sets right through although in Year 9 when I chose manufacturing as a GCSE the school tried to talk me out of it. They said it was more for children who were not academic, but it was something I really wanted to do. I didn't want to study German or

French. I thought I like making things, so maybe I'll make something. Most of the kids in the manufacturing class were a lot of the naughtier kids. I enjoyed this class and in the summer we built petrol go-karts with roll cages and stuff on and the teacher said to us if we worked hard then the first lesson next week we'll go down the field and we'll get to go and play on the go-karts. So we worked solid because we wanted to, and you didn't hear a whisper in the classroom.

Clearly I had an attitude at secondary school. You'd get a teacher saying right do this, and I would say no, why should I. They would say you were adults but would treat you like kids, that the bell was for them and not for me, and having to put your hand up to talk just makes you think you are back at primary school in carpet time. Half way through Year 9 I also started to bunk off school. In the last couple of years my mum would drag me up to the school and actually watch me walk in the door and then I would just literally walk straight out and I'd be about ten metres behind my mum as she walked home, and I'd be walking down to meet my mates. The school would phone home automatically if the computer records showed I was absent but that was not a problem for me, I would just go into school and change the register so that I could be at home for the next week – the school computers were not a problem.

When I look back I think that perhaps the school did as much as they could to be honest. There's only one person's choice and it was mine. I was part of a group whom the school saw as troublesome. We weren't like the bullies, just a group, we knew everyone, but we were the ones who were always cheeky, the ones always thinking of doing stupid stuff. They tried splitting us up. They tried to give us detentions but they never used to work. You'd get ten minutes after class, and if you didn't turn up for that one you'd get an hour detention, and if you didn't turn up for that one you'd get an hour and a half with the headmaster, and if you don't turn up for that they exclude you and give you a day off! So that's what we used to do, have a day off!

I was always bigger than most of the teachers in the school and they were intimidated. My learning mentor tried to get me to understand the effect I had on people and would say that when I got into a fight and went absolutely mad, he said a lot of the teachers would not want to get close to me because they felt frightened. I was mostly a calm sort of person but when I do sort of flip out a bit, then people do stay away from me. My family's quite open but I keep everything to myself and then I'll boil up and then someone can just say something little to me and I'll flip out.

My dad died when I was 15, but I had never really known him. When my mum and dad got divorced I was only three months old and then I didn't meet my dad again all through primary and secondary school until I was aged 13. My older sister had gone to the doctors and she rang me immediately and said, 'I've met our dad at the GP's surgery, come up and meet him' and I was like OK and put the phone down and carried on just watching the TV. So I watched, the programme not sort of sinking in, and then I hobbled, I had a broken ankle at the time from falling out of a tree, and went off to the doctors and met him. It was strange because he was like my dad but he wasn't sort of thing and then we saw him every weekend, and then it faded out and I hadn't seen him since. Then I found out that he had died. He had blocked arteries to the heart from prolonged use of cocaine and smoking weed. But I don't think that it affected me. It made me not care about anything, and I think that was the point where I just give up caring. And I give up really worrying about teachers bothering me and stuff. I don't think my school ever knew about my dad.

Reflections
When school finished for everyone I sussed that I need a job and I went to this firm just filling boxes and cages six hours a day for three months. It was for the minimum wage – I absolutely hated it. I left this job and went to work in a shop selling motor accessories which I enjoyed. It paid £4 an hour, but I didn't get on with the people and then a mate found me a job up by the airport fitting tyres and stuff in a garage. And now I am working again in a shop selling motor accessories.

Soon as I left school I started to regret about things. I wanted to go back to school and redo my last few years. I absolutely hate to think about how I messed those last few years up – how I messed up considering I was at school for 13 years, 13 years is a long time and two years out of thirteen is no time whatsoever. I hate the jobs I do now, they're all sort of minimum wage and you've got to work so hard to climb up the ladder from the bottom when I could have gone in halfway up to the top already. I might have done a management course or something. It seems too late now. I've got a lot of commitments with my money now and if I went to college I don't think I could financially afford it. I thought well if I do go back to college I'll try and sort out the financials this year and then next year I can go back to college. But I don't think I'll do it, I'll just carry on working.

I have always wanted to go back to school and sort of try to explain to people that they will regret things if they don't try and make it work. But it is so hard to try and get this across to people. For myself I have always not wanted to be a stat. I didn't just want to be another number in the Government's eyes, I wanted to be my own person but to me all I am is another cog in the machine. I always wanted not to be a cog in the machine. I wanted to be the driver if you know what I mean. I've never wanted to work for payday, I've always just wanted to work and work because I wanted to work.

Harry achieved a Level 3 in English, a Level 4 in mathematics, and a Level 5 in science at Key Stage 2. At secondary school at Key Stage 3 he achieved a Level 3 in English, a level 6 in mathematics, and a Level 5 in science. He did not take any GCSE examinations.

Jackie's story

I attended one primary school and did occasionally skive. I was always quite nervous of school and sometimes I would say to my mum that I was unwell. I never bunked off at primary school, just skived. My mum sort of believed that I was not well but my dad didn't believe it. I was kind of a mummy's girl so she didn't get too cross but my dad was stricter and would ground us and stuff if we did things wrong.

I enjoyed most of my primary school, although I know that I could have done better. I really wanted to please my teachers. And in Year 3 we used to do songs every day because the teacher played the guitar – we used to finish every day with a song. I enjoyed singing then but not now. I did not get any problems at primary school and I was keen on learning. What made me keen was that the work was fun and easy to do. In primary school I was happy to learn, everyone was, we were all alike, friends, we were good.

I was nervous about going to secondary school. When I got there I found that the work was harder and I started to hang around with people in Year 7 who were getting into trouble. We did everything we could to upset the teachers – swearing at them, not doing our work. We used to sit in a line at the back of our history class and just hum, and this would annoy the teacher and we'd sit there humming until we got kicked out of the class and then we'd go round the school knocking on other classes. We used to run about the corridors. It was the way to make friends. I didn't want to be seen as a keener but when I look back on it now I wished I had done my work. Whoever was keen to learn, they just got picked on and called names and bullied – keeners. I didn't even know what that word keener meant until I got to secondary school.

I didn't skive from secondary school I just bunked off. My mum used to take me to school in the mornings, and I'd go through the front gates and then out the back gates and I'd go up into the woods and then we'd go on Woodstock View as everyone called it. We'd stay up there all day just messing about. Then at lunchtime if we did not have our packed lunch we'd go into school and get our dinner, go in for afternoon registration and come back out again. Sometimes we would register in the morning but not always. They must have noticed but never seemed to do anything about it. My mum and dad wanted me to be at school but in the end there was nothing they could do to make me go. When I think about the reasons why we bunked off so much I think it was because my friends were doing it and it was more fun than lessons. And sometimes I did it because I had fallen out with people and I was worried about being beaten up.

So sometimes I didn't go to school because I was just too scared. And it was even your friends who turned on you. I just tagged along with the hard people to try and get myself friends. I got beat up out of school by girls from another school and my so-called friends from my school didn't do anything to help me. It happened at the fairground by the school and it was about 5 o'clock and I was on a ride. I managed to phone my mum and ask her to come and pick me up, and then I got off the ride and 15 girls just came and beat me up. And I had to go to hospital and the hospital said that if I had had another couple of kicks to the head I would have gone into a coma. I knew who the ringleaders were and the police were involved but they were only given a warning. I was 13 when this happened to me.

When I went back to school after this, because a lot of them had seen me being beaten up, they thought 'she isn't going to do anything' and they kept getting at me and trying to pick fights with me which I didn't want and so in the end I just didn't go to school. The school did not support me when I went back. No they didn't do anything. You'd go and tell the teacher and they'd say 'Oh if you are getting picked on come and tell us and we'll sort it out' but they didn't, they don't, they don't do anything. I used to think that the teachers were just as bad as the kids. Sometimes they were so distressed by the kids that they got upset and cried. I think that a lot of the teachers were scared and when I saw some of the women teachers crying I thought they should not be teachers, they were not strong enough. If I was a teacher or a headteacher I would have expelled these naughty kids but they got away with it.

So I told my mum that I wouldn't go back to school and I began to throw tantrums. In the end they gave up and I didn't go back and I stayed at home for about a year and a half. The welfare never came round, and I wasn't offered any tuition. After a bit I asked my mum to try and get me some work from school that I could do at home. They sent me back two books, I think, and I did the homework and sent it into the school for marks, and it didn't ever get marked and I didn't ever hear any more about homework.

Over the next year things got worse for me and I used to meet up with older mates or some of those not going to school and we would drink and smoke and stuff like that. We'd usually drink cider because it was cheapest and I'd probably drink about one and half litres a night sometimes more than that unless we were smoking weed as well. We'd go up the private area, where the private houses were, and drink and then we would go about the place when we were drunk and be all loud.

When I was 15 something changed and I got fed up of staying home and wanted to go to a different school. The new school was quite a long way away and my mum would take me every morning. It seemed a lot better, there wasn't any fighting and people were easy to get to know and get along with. The work was all right as well. But then I only managed to stay at this school for a term. I was still drinking a lot at this time in the evening and I would get to school with hangovers and in the end I just wanted to give up school and hang around with my mates. The drinking and smoking were too much and I didn't have enough willpower to say no to it and so I just gave up everything to drink.

After that I tried going to college but I didn't want to go to any round Bristol in case there was anyone there I might know from school. Then I met my boyfriend and I thought well I'll try and go to college in a couple of years. I got a job recently as a sales assistant, but I am expecting a baby and my health has not been good enough for me to carry on working.

Reflections

I don't know what happens between primary and secondary school. Certainly at secondary school there were more people who were not keen to work than there were people who were keen. Basically I was scared to be keen to work in case I got picked on.

Things are different now, I have a boyfriend and I don't drink anymore. I am applying for jobs and when I fill in the application forms, because I have no qualifications, I don't say I was picked on, I just write that I was really immature but I've grown up a lot since. The only people I have spoken to about this before are my family and my boyfriend – I don't tell anyone about it because I am more ashamed than anything. I've been able to tell about it today but I had to make sure that it was all like to one person in one room before I could do it. I wouldn't have done this if it had been in a group.

Jackie achieved a Level 4 grade in each of English, mathematics and science at the end of primary school. She did not take any further tests or attempt GCSE examinations at secondary school.

Devlin's story

I went to three primary schools. We first had to move because my mum met a partner. She had just had a child with him, and he wanted us to move to the other side of the city. I was eight years old at the time, and my sister was ten. After just five weeks in this new house and school my mum and her new partner split up and we had to move back and stay with my auntie and this meant going to yet another primary school and another house. It was bad timing because at school it was like two or three different kinds of stuff to manage. It was quite difficult for me to get used to the big changes and things.

I don't really make a lot of friends and if I'm not in a school for very long it's difficult. At the third primary school I made one certain friend and then that's it. But I did manage to get results before I went to secondary school with Level 4 grades in English and mathematics. This was good really as I had real difficulties with my eyesight all through primary school and that affected my reading and writing and it didn't get recognised and sorted out until I was nine years old. Then a teacher, Mrs Croft, she was like a special needs teacher, noticed that I found it difficult to see properly and I needed glasses for reading small print and obviously my handwriting was not that good so she helped me to improve it.

So going to secondary school was obviously an easy move because I was used to changing over to different things. But then again I did have trouble settling in. Sometimes I couldn't do the work and stuff and most things just went wrong, 'cos I became like more dangerous and things. I got picked on and I'd end up going to hit someone and if someone shouts at me then normally I'd go for them, so that's why for most of the time I was either suspended or having a bit of time off so I could stop myself from doing things that I didn't want to do. But the main problem started in Year 10 and in the groups I was in there was lots of shouting and I couldn't concentrate and would end up shouting back, then getting told off and then getting put out of class.

So I would be trying to do my work but I can't do it if I'm not in the classroom to do it.

I needed teachers who knew me, who knew what I could do. I did have a Learning Mentor, his name was Peter and he'd say that if I wanted to go to him then all I had to do was to walk out of the class. Because of all this stuff happening I wouldn't want to work or do anything and I'd just try and hold myself back from doing something, and I would try to do things to calm myself down a bit. It was then that the Learning Mentor was a help – I could go to him. If I spoke to him he would keep things confidential. He came for home visits. He also used to sit with me in class sometimes and he'd help me understand the work. But he was off for quite a while with ill health and he had to stay off and so I didn't have anyone after that. I did not see him just before he went but he sent me a letter in the post personally, to say that he was off.

By the time he returned I had already been excluded. It all seemed to go very wrong after Key Stage 3. When I got put out of school for good it was because of a time with a teacher who was strict, wanted you to do your work and if you didn't do it she would do you for it. But this time I was pushed into her desk and I knocked some work off the desk and it all got messed up so I said I would help pick it up, and I did this and she was fine about it. But then this other kid put it in the bin and then messed it up and the teacher thought it was me and she threw me out of the class. She pulled me and I pushed her and she hit her wrist on the door handle and in the end I went completely mad and just started hitting her and things. I was angry at the other kid for putting the work in the bin and then with her for putting me out of the class. She bruised her rib on the door and she had a cut on her face. It was a difficult time.

After being put out of school I was put on a ten-week course in Year 10 at college on business studies, which I enjoyed because the groups were small, and I could get on and concentrate on my work. But for the rest of the summer term in Year 10 and all through Year 11 I did no schooling at all. I wanted to carry on after the ten-week course and to stay in the same place because I knew it, and was settled there. A student used to come and help me, her name was Sarah, but she wasn't there for that long because she got moved to somewhere else.

I didn't really talk with my mum about all these difficulties – she used to ask sometimes about certain things and stuff but it wasn't exactly often. I'm more a person who does things than talks about them. My mum and sister do the talking. And my dad left my mum when I was only just a year old. He stays in touch a bit with my mum. But I don't really know him. And then of course my step-dad left when I was about nine. I'm the one who does things in the house, sorting out and fixing things. I'm there to deal with it, I'm meant to be the man in the house and if jobs need doing then I'll just go and do it.

Reflections

I have been sad. I was sad when the Learning Mentor left because I was used to him being there. He used to help quite a lot. I was sad at the end of a day if I had been teased a lot and if someone had said something to me, and there was no one I could go to. The headteacher never used to help anyone, my head of year, well he just didn't like me anyway so I didn't bother going to him 'cos I knew he won't do nothing, so there wasn't anyone really I could go to. I felt isolated.

Devlin achieved a Level 4 for both English and mathematics and a Level 3 for science at Key Stage 2. He did not take Key Stage 3 tests or GCSE examinations at secondary school.

What was it that made it so hard for these young people to achieve GCSE qualifications, fulfil their academic potential and have any sense of engagement and enjoyment from their secondary schooling? What was it in their family lives that made this so difficult? What kind of school settings might have enabled them to be more successful? What kind of training, resources, school design and organisation would have supported teachers to be better able to address their needs?

Hearing the whole story

As I listened to the stories of young people like Kirsten, Harry, Jackie and Devlin, I became concerned not only for the hurt they expressed but for my own ignorance. I had worked for over 30 years in education, 16 of these as a headteacher of large secondary schools, but how little I had really known of the full stories of these disaffected and difficult to engage young people.

It is possible as a headteacher to know parts of the story: the Year 11 boy unable to cry at the death of his grandmother; a child in panic terrified even to contemplate ten minutes in school; the anger of the pupil who is put out into the corridor every lesson regardless of his behaviour; the concerns expressed in the school council about levels of bullying; the exhaustion of staff as they try to foster commitment and engagement from unwilling youngsters; my own attempts to hold and contain the staff's anxiety as we struggled to foster maturity in what seemed like at times a challenging sea of adolescence.

However, the fuller story, including the family story, is seldom heard by the school; and the school story becomes a series of events to which the school is compelled to respond rather than a narrative of information which might help to enable the young person to engage. Stories like these carry very significant messages for policy makers, headteachers and practitioners about the design of settings we provide for less resilient young people who attend our mainstream secondary schools.

What we can learn from these stories?

Themes that emerge from these narratives include:

- a sharp contrast between the experience of academic success at primary school and failure to achieve any qualifications at secondary school, resulting in feelings of shame and regret, internalised disappointment and inadequacy;
- a lack of resilience in managing secondary school settings, leading to self exclusion often from as early as 14;
- a lack of safe, consistent and reliable support in secondary school, which is experienced as a place not of community but of violence, fear and regulation;
- discontinuity, with multiple changes in family and school settings and little in the way of permanence in relationships to provide a sense of being noticed and known;
- a feeling of isolation both at home and at school; and
- the loss of significant others in their lives and a hurt, so often unexpressed, carried in relation to fathers who have left or have never really been known.

These stories show how limited is the ability of secondary schools to address the needs of young people with complex social, emotional and cognitive challenges, especially where numbers of disengaged pupils reach a critical mass. Indeed it would seem the size, design and organisation of secondary schools actually exacerbates the difficulties they face. 'Self exclusion' from another viewpoint might be seen as institutional exclusion, with the practices of our schools making it impossible to provide socially and educationally inclusive settings for the disaffected and difficult to engage young. As one experienced primary school teacher put it to me having read the stories of Harry, Kirsten and the others: 'It is not the children who are failing in our schools, but the structure and processes of the system to meet their needs.'

These stories underline a key finding of the *Holding Children in Mind over Time* report: that disaffected young people who fail to thrive in school often demonstrate the consequences of poor attachment experiences arising from the quality of relationships with significant others at key times during childhood.[42] Aspects of poverty, drug use, and family breakdown are also implicated in the narratives, and the result is that 'poverty of affection' impacts on both learner identities and a young person's ability to cope with their schooling experience. My question is, if poor attachment experiences have such dire consequences, what impact should attachment theory have on the design of our schools?

We will look at the implications of attachment theory in Chapter Four, but first we need to call to mind one theme that arose from the young peoples' narratives in this chapter. There was a telling contrast between the experience of academic success at primary school and failure to achieve any qualifications at secondary school. Kirsten, Harry, Jackie and Devlin recalled teachers in their primary schools with whom they built and developed long-term and comfortable relationships. Such supportive and important relationships were possible in part because teachers could really 'get to know' their pupils and the pupils learn to trust and depend upon these respected adults. I would argue that these kinds of relationships are only possible where there is consistent contact between teachers and pupils, where unhelpful change is kept to a minimum and where teachers and pupils see a lot of each other during each school day. These are 'human scale' relationships, only possible where the unit of social experience is relatively small and stable. It is to the lessons we can learn from the implications of human scale that we next turn.

Summary

- Four young people share their stories of family and school life in Bristol. All left primary school with Level 4 grades in English, mathematics and/or science at Key Stage 2, but took no GCSE examinations at the end of their secondary schooling.
- A number of themes emerge from the testimonies of the disaffected and difficult to engage young:
  - a sharp contrast between the experience of academic success at primary school and failure to achieve any qualifications at secondary school, resulting in feelings of shame and regret, internalised disappointment and inadequacy;
  - a lack of resilience in managing secondary school settings, leading to self exclusion often from as early as 14;
  - a lack of safe, consistent and reliable support in secondary school, which is experienced as a place not of community but of violence, fear and regulation;
  - discontinuity, with multiple changes in family and school settings and little in the way of permanence in relationships to provide a sense of being noticed and known;
  - a feeling of isolation both at home and at school; and
  - the loss of significant others in their lives and a hurt, so often unexpressed, carried in relation to fathers who have left or have never really been known.
- Schools seldom hear the whole story, including the family story; they respond to incidents without information which might help to enable the young person to engage.
- The ability of secondary schools to address the needs of young people with complex social, emotional and cognitive challenges is limited, especially where numbers of the disaffected reach a critical mass. The size, design and organisation of secondary schools exacerbate the problem.

CHAPTER THREE
Learning from human scale international practice

'It's exhausting work at best. Still we dare not rest until we can look about and say that there is not a *single* school to which we would not willingly – I don't say gladly, just willingly – send our own children. Small self-governing public schools are the quickest and most efficient route to that end.'

Deborah Meier, *The Power of Their Ideas* (1995)[43]

Early history of the small school movement in the USA

By the 1970s school size had become an issue in the United States and by the 1980s two educational reformers had begun to question whether large comprehensive high schools were now obsolete, 'designed for another time, and far out of sync with the demands of our diverse republic'.[44] Ernest Boyer, President of the Carnegie Foundation for the Advancement of Teaching, identified the size and impersonality of comprehensive high schools as a primary source of the alienation and apathy he found among students, whilst Ted Sizer, former Dean of the Harvard Graduate School of Education, recommended that such schools be reshaped into smaller educational settings.[45]

Sizer went on to pioneer the small school movement in the United States. With Debbie Meier, he established Central Park East Secondary School in Harlem, New York, in 1985. Their collaboration was pivotal. Meier was not only a school and community leader but also a school designer attending to the detailed implications of her ideas. She went back to basic questions: how children learn, how classes work, what needs to change and why.

Innovations at Central Park East Secondary School

Meier was convinced that size was the single most important change that needed to be made. Size was a pre-condition without which other aspects of the programme would be unmanageable. Size was an organising principle at Central Park East Secondary School. One criterion was whether the whole school community could fit into the auditorium; another, whether the staff could all sit face to face in a single circle. The community should be small enough for all students to know each other – there should be no strangers.

Meier argued that small schools could be more efficient and effective and had the ability to make changes quickly; they were not preoccupied with complex timetabling; innovations did not become a Herculean task requiring a great bureaucracy; accountability was a matter of access and not a complex machinery through distanced governing bodies.

Curriculum innovations at Central Park East included the intro-duction of two-hour interdisciplinary class periods, which provided time for presentations, seminars, group work and independent study. Meier saw the need to build in time for tutorials and coaching. She also thought critically about the load on teachers and their relationship with children. Teachers at Central Park East were rarely responsible for more than 40 children a day (two groups) and stayed with these pupils for two years. Another key design principle was to keep the schedule simple so that teachers could concentrate on the complexity of the children and the complexity of the ideas they were working with.

The Boston Pilot Schools

Meier's work in New York foreshadowed the development of the Pilot School movement in Boston. In 1995 a unique partnership between the city's mayor, the school committee, the education superintendent and the teachers' union set up Pilot Schools to serve as laboratories of innovation, and research and development sites for effective urban public (i.e. state-funded) schools. Written into the Boston Pilot Schools teachers' union contract is a telling aspiration:

'The purpose of establishing Pilot Schools is to provide models of educational excellence that will help to foster widespread educational reform throughout all Boston Public Schools.'

The Pilot Schools have four essential features in common:

- autonomy: the schools have greater freedom over staffing, budget, curriculum and assessment, governance, and timetable than other Boston state schools;
- accountability: the schools are held to higher levels of accounta-bility in exchange for increased autonomy;
- a 'human scale' size: the schools are small enough for students and adults to know each other well, typically enrolling fewer than 400 students, and their mission is to create 'nurturing environments' in which staff attend to the learning needs of all students;

● a commitment to equality: these schools are non selective and strive to enrol students representative of the entire district.

'Human scale' is essential but not sufficient

Of the four essential features of the Pilot Schools the critical issue of school size was what most strongly differentiated opinions as the movement developed. For some it was a core design principle, for others it was seen as useful but not a pre-condition for successful schooling. So what are current American school leaders saying? In interviews for the *Dispatches* programme, 'The Children Left Behind', Ann Cook, Headteacher at Urban Academy in New York, Linda Nathan, Headteacher at Boston Arts Academy, and Peggy Kemp, Headteacher at Fenway High in Boston, all emphasised that whilst it was essential for schools to be small, this in itself was not sufficient. What was important were the opportunities that being a small learning community gave schools in terms of relationships, pedagogy, curriculum and assessment.[46]

Putting relationships at the heart

Linda Nathan identifies a focus on relationships as being absolutely central for successful schooling. At first sight this may sound simplistic, but its implications are transformational. In the UK typically a teacher in a large comprehensive school will teach 250 children a week. By contrast in some of the Boston Pilot Schools no teacher sees more than 75 students and no student more than four teachers a week. This reduction in teacher to student contact has far-reaching implications for the design and organisation of the school and a significant impact on the shape of the curriculum. This in turn influences the way teaching and learning can be approached; and thus how teachers should be trained and supported.

Further, it is clear from my field visits to the Boston Pilot Schools that teachers have found that 'human scale' schools have allowed them to renew their passion for their work, meeting as a professional group of not more than 25 practitioners to think together, and to design curriculum and assessment approaches that are relevant, intellectually challenging and engaging. The size of the schools has also allowed teachers to talk with each other on a daily basis about which children are not fully engaged in learning and make immediate responses to address their needs.

Qualities needed for teaching in small schools

Meier made strong demands on teachers. She did not believe that urban education was easy. She identified the challenges, 'three tough things', which teachers had to do in this new environment. The first was to change how they viewed learning itself; second, to develop new habits of mind; and third, to develop habits of working which were collegial. She felt that too many teachers were 'passion impaired' and she had clear views on the qualities needed for teaching in small schools. Teachers must demonstrate the capacity for self-conscious reflection on how and why they were able to learn; sympathy for others; a willingness to work collaboratively; a passion for having someone else share their interests; perseverance, energy and a devotion to getting things right. She argued that American education would only change if all schools were educationally inspiring and intellectually challenging for teachers, and job satisfaction was anchored in intellectual growth.

Thoughtful schools with reflective practitioners

The design and organisation of schools is not only a technical issue but also a philosophical question – what sort of school community are we trying to create? The small schools that Meier founded were self-governing and pedagogically interesting. They were schools with a focus and a philosophy, where staff came together around common ideas, and all this within the public education system.

This highlights significant issues to do with teachers' professional identities. In my field visits to Boston between 2003 and 2008 I did not get a feeling that there was prescription about how things should be done within small schools, rather that there was an opportunity for professionals to think, talk and shape the learning environments that they were part of.

Meier wanted to create what she called 'thoughtful schools' – and 'thoughtfulness' was resourced and built into the design and practice of the community. Meier acknowledged that this was time-consuming. She also provided teachers with the conditions where they could work collaboratively and again noted that collaboration was time-consuming. Rather than seeing time as a budget line, Meier engineered settings where thinking and collaboration could occur as part of the process and practice of the school.

Meier wanted to create schools in which consensus was easy to arrive at but where argument and discussion about teaching and learning could be encouraged. The smallness of the school allowed the staff to meet around a table, in a circle, perhaps at short notice, to address an issue or to plan for the longer term. Staff development was enhanced by continuous dialogue, face to face, about how things could be done better, how the staff group could make improvements that were in line with the philosophy of the school and would make a difference for the students.

Bringing the community together at a moment's notice

Size makes a difference in other ways too. At times of drama or concern – for instance when there is a rumour of a fight, of drug use, a family crisis, students running away from home – it is possible to bring the school together at a moment's notice and talk through the ways in which such matters might be managed and how the values and the ethos of the school can be maintained. Staff can spend time on this not because they are more caring than teachers in large schools but because they are working in a structure, and with a style, that enables them to show that care more effectively.

When I reflect on my experience of leading and managing large schools over 16 years, I am exhausted to think of what we had to do to bring the whole school community together. In my first headship of a secondary school in Wiltshire, with a student body of around 1,100 students, we were able to bring the whole school together in the sports hall. However, as important as it was for the school community to meet together in this way, we only attempted it at the end of each term. This was not a philosophical decision about fre-quency, but a practical one, in that it took almost half a day to orchestrate the safe and orderly gathering. But when we were all there, with the school orchestra, and the student and staff choirs, and we shared ritual that carried meaning, these gatherings were critically important to the health of the school as a community. I can remember my last experience of this as I came to leave the school, and a sixth form student, who had been on an exchange visit to India that I had lead, sang the 'Pie Jesu' from Faure's *Requiem* unaccompanied and her voiced soared over 1,100 young people, there were many who were moved to tears, including me.

In my second headship in Bristol, in a school of nearly 1300 pupils, there was not even a sports hall to allow the whole school to meet together, and at the end of each term or at moments of crisis or loss or celebration, when it was necessary to speak to the whole school, it required six assemblies/gatherings to be held through a morning to share a message of importance with everyone present. In some schools the only time that the community gathers is when there is a fire drill!

Transmission of culture, values and life skills

For Meier, schooling is a part of the process of child rearing. Schools need to be small enough, she argues, that we can attend to each other's funerals as well as confirmations, notice birthdays and weddings, as well as haircuts and new suits.

Meier also believed that our schools should be the place where society expresses itself to all young people about what really matters. For her this meant that schools should be designed and organised in such a way as to immerse students in a culture that adults had had a significant part in shaping. She felt that adult and student cultures rarely interconnected in large high schools.

In a world where the transmission of values, culture, and life skills is often not part of the family's role, and where young people are no longer 'apprenticed', our schools may be the last and perhaps only place where this can happen. However, in large schools the issue of control and the imperatives of targets often mean that there is no complex and powerful counterculture to balance the one that is currently being offered to young people, pressurising them to be consumers within a fragmented and individualised society rather than citizens within a community.

There seems to be no counterforce representing adult ideas and concerns which young people might know and understand and then apprentice themselves to. Yet this goes to the very heart of why teachers become teachers – to bring to children a set of adult intellectual standards and appreciations. As Meier puts it with such passion – it is the central task of adults to share with young people a 'love affair with literature and history, and science and mathematics, logic and reason, accuracy and precision, as well as the commitment to justice and fairness'.[47]

This connects strongly with deeply problematic and competing discourses shaping English education at this time – especially the promotion of vocational skills and an agenda of economic competitiveness in a globalised world, which sees young people from 14 years onwards as proto workers in business and industry.

Education researcher and writer Lynn Raphael Reed describes how the schools currently being built in the UK 'look like call centres or IT open offices; their students wear uniforms which are like corporate badges; and much of the competency curricula that is being adopted by schools erases all references to community...'[48]

Raphael Reed argues that to some extent: 'this dominant discourse is in tension with the Children's agenda (as represented by Every Child Matters) and the Community agenda (as encapsulated in the duty to promote community cohesion).'[49] The new philosophy is a 'predominantly functionalist and utilitarian model for state education (far removed from either the liberal model enshrined in much private education in Britain or in the more radical models as captured in the Boston Schools)'.

But if we want children to be caring and compassionate then we must provide a place for growing up in which they can themselves experience care and compassion. This is what I call the importance of learning in and through community, and why the 'school community' is so important, being perhaps the only or last place for young people to develop the community understanding through experience which they can take into their adult lives.

Learning from the Danish educational system

The most significant review of educational provision in Denmark arose out of a national 'conversation' in the early 1990s. Its findings were enshrined in the Folkeskole Act of 1994, which emphasised a national collective responsibility for the education and wellbeing of its young people.

The Folkeskole Act promoted the design of a 12-year comprehensive school experience for all children, with a commitment to:

- a socially relevant curriculum;
- interdisciplinary and project-orientated approaches to learning;
- the abolition of setting by ability in classes;
- education as an enterprise linking home and school; and
- school accountability to the local community.

Another notable feature of the Danish system is a variety which not only offers choice but also ensures that all students can be supported in an educational setting that is designed to meet their needs, is well resourced, and has status. There seems to be a determination for education provision to be socially and educationally inclusive – there is somewhere for everyone to go that has credibility and esteem in the eyes of young people and their families.

The Folkeskole

In Denmark there are no transition difficulties as primary and secondary provision is integrated into one Folkeskole (school) for all children aged from six to 16, with no more than 500 students in a school. In practice this means a two-form entry throughout. There are nine years of compulsory education with an optional additional year at age 16; children are divided into groups by age, but not by ability; and progression from one year to the next is automatic.

Assessment is continuous and formative, and teachers are encouraged not to give their students marks until Grade 8 (when they are 14 years of age). Pedagogy is based on group work, learning together. Final certification at the end of the Folkeskole is seen as a statement of the school's relationship to the student. The assessments are based on achievements in Danish, mathematics, English, German, physics and chemistry. There is also a final-year project to be completed. The final assessment is given as a written statement and the publication of final marks is at the request of the student.

School reputation is not linked to examination results but to school atmosphere, the quality of school life for the pupils, the quality of relationships between teachers and pupils, and the quality of learning.

The key person for all students is the Klasslaerer (form teacher) who stays with the group all the way though the school to the age of 16, providing an emotional backbone of attachment for the students and their families on their journey through school to young adulthood.

The class group is often more important to the student than the school. It remains the same through to Grade 9 so that the students have continuity both with their subject teachers and their class group. The relative structural stability of the class group has important implications for the child's experience of school as a safe, reliable and consistent setting. Long-term class and teacher continuity are seen as key requirements for individual pupil wellbeing and achievement.

Danish teachers have a four-year training in the Seminarium and are expected to teach three or four subjects. A major focus of teacher training is on child development and the skills and approaches that enable a teacher to build class atmosphere and a sense of community in their school.

The Efterskole

Efterskoles are also known as continuation schools and are especially intended for young people over 14 years of age. They are boarding schools and the state and municipality contribute to boarding and tuition costs. There are Efterskoles throughout Denmark and many have a special focus, for example, sport, music, languages or the environment. Many pupils choose an Efterskole in order to gain independence as well as having the opportunity to live and learn in a community. They provide a one-year experience for young people at an important time in their adolescence.

One of the Efterskoles I visited on a field visit to Denmark was Ollerup Efterskole, sang og music (song and music), in Funen. It was exceptionally well appointed and resourced. It catered for 130 students who all had an aptitude for music and singing and who would spend the year not only covering the curriculum they would have had at the Folkeskole but also being supported and challenged to reach levels of excellence in individual and group performance. Students were involved in running the community, and joined housekeeping and catering teams as a regular commitment to their involvement.

It is not hard to imagine the benefit of such an experience for young people from urban settings as a one-year option on their school journey. What impresses about the Danish system is the flexibility, the range of possibilities and the level of resource that is made available.

Year 10 Klasseskole, Albertslund in Copenhagen

The tenth year at a Folkeskole is voluntary. At Albertslund, students do not stay at their original Folkeskole but go to a separate stand alone school set in the middle of one of the most challenging districts in Copenhagen. The school caters for 160 students in one-storey buildings that have been designed to create a sense of calm and space. It is a dedicated centre for vocational diploma work, with a mix of core subjects and vocational options linked to external placements and work internships. Students improve their qualifications in order to be eligible for training or education options that will meet their needs, but the school is more than just a pathway to vocational training. There is a strong sense of this being a community of learners with an emphasis on induction, counselling support, academic and vocational courses, and ritual and graduation. The 'human scale' of the setting makes all this personal for each student and demand for places is high. The school is exceptionally well cared for and resourced. It is not a poor alternative to an academic school but an impressive example of the possibilities of vocational education and the support particular students might need between the end of the Folkeskole and college or further training.

Are small schools more effective?

A recent evaluation of the Pilot Schools in Boston carried out by the Center for Collaborative Education reflected that:

> 'Taken together the student engagement and the performance findings show that the Pilot School students are outperforming the district average on a range of behaviours and academics.'[50]

The evaluation questioned whether the Pilot Schools' conditions of smallness and autonomy over resources did actually improve student engagement and performance. The findings showed that the schools:

- ranked highest amongst Boston Public Schools for attendance, reflecting high levels of engagement by students;
- had the longest waiting list of any Boston public schools and that their desirability had increased over time, signalling an attraction to Boston families for small, personalised schools;
- had the lowest suspension rates of all Boston public schools, indicating that they were safe places to learn and achieve;
- achieved comparably better than the city average in the Massachusetts's State tests for mathematics and English;
- had both high rates of graduation and the highest rates of students going onto college within the Boston public school system.

But are small schools affordable?

One of the essential tenets of the Pilot School movement was that it should provide models of innovation within the overall system and that the knowledge it created would be available to all schools in the city, but that dollar for dollar it would not be more expensive. When asked if Pilot Schools were affordable, Peggy Kemp, Headteacher at Fenway High School in Boston, replied that they were 'a lot more affordable than the criminal justice system'.

Indeed, graduate for graduate it is argued that small schools are cheaper than other state schools – particularly when you add into the equation additional costs that would have to be met by the state to respond to drop outs and the increased drug prevention programmes, teacher turnover and burn out, vandalism, security measures, and, for those who give up the challenge of engaging with civil society, social benefit and custodial costs.

And small schools do not necessarily miss out on the economies of scale. In a system of small schools in close proximity to each other, nothing prevents schools from agreeing to collaborate to offer specialised courses, or joining together to create sports teams and choirs and orchestras, or sharing facilities. Fenway High School and Boston Arts Academy are two separate schools, for instance, yet share a very substantial library and resource centre, a canteen, and a school hall, and all this in converted industrial buildings.

How successful is the Folkeskole system?

Empirical evidence is thin on the ground. There are small pieces of research that show that although pupils in different European countries share many common concerns, they also come to school with significantly different attitudes towards themselves as learners, towards school and towards achievement. As a result their expectations of themselves and of their teachers are also different. In this context, Danish schools are doing well.[51] They also do comparatively well in relation to the development of young people as independent learners. Schools in Denmark seem better able to manage crucial transitions in the responsibilities for academic study, from the early experience of dependency on teachers, in primary years, to the construction of independent learner goals in the later phases of secondary education in anticipation of the greater degree of autonomy required in tertiary and continuing education.[52]

In 2001 the *European Report on the Quality of School Education* chose 'drop-out rates from secondary education' (i.e. the percentage of population aged 18–24 not in employment, education or training) as one of the 16 quality indicators. The report showed that drop-out rates remain relatively high in the EU, at an average of 22.5 per cent. There are, however, notable differences between member states. The data suggest that the northern states are better at combating the phenomenon of drop-out from secondary schooling than other states. Portugal (40.7 per cent), Italy (30.2 per cent), Spain (30.0 per cent) and the United Kingdom (31.4 per cent) show alarmingly high drop-out rates, whilst in Denmark it is 12.5 per cent. The report comments:

> 'The better scores of some northern countries, for instance, are often attributed to the organisation of their educational systems, in the sense that the less selective mechanisms in education systems such as the integrated Nordic model could help to ease the transition between different school environments when a pupil moves from primary to secondary level.'[53]

Some might argue that this is old data – almost a decade old – but there is no evidence that any other European surveys have superseded these findings. What the 2001 European Commission report suggests is that it is the organisation of the education system in each country that has a profound effect on young people's attitudes to and engagement with their secondary schooling.

Paradigm shift needed in school organisation

The legacy of our own current system presents some real difficulties in any future move to smaller schools – with the development of teachers as subject specialists, with the career ladder of heads of departments and faculty leaders, with headteacher salaries and pensions linked to school size, with the structures and systems that we have come to know and accept within our schools as they are currently designed and organised.

Any policy shift towards smaller schools will be a complex and challenging affair and one that will need to look not only at the implications for change to the deep-seated habitual practices and behaviours of those who work in schools, the practitioners, but will also challenge researchers to work in new ways, those whose role it is to regulate and inspect schools, and in particular those at university level involved with the training and development of teachers. This is not a simple question of downsizing or dividing up big schools. Creating small schools is a paradigm shift, which will test every educational nerve, sinew and muscle of our current system.

The examples we have explored from the USA and Denmark show how much there might be gained from such a shift. Being small enough to be human scale is considered essential but not sufficient to ensure young people can make a successful childhood. Being human scale is essential but so is understanding that many factors that contribute to a successful childhood are associated with long-term 'deep' interpersonal relationships between children and a small number of significant adults. Such relationships are based on important psychological and developmental theories of attachment. In the next chapter we will consider the implications of attachment theory for ensuring successful childhoods for many more of our young people.

Summary

- What lessons can be learned from abroad? This chapter considers the small school movement in the USA and the education system in Denmark.
- The small school movement started in the USA in the 1970s and 80s when education reformers began to question the efficacy of large comprehensive high schools.
- In 1985 Ted Sizer and Debbie Meier established the Central Park East Secondary School in Harlem, where size was an organising principle: teachers saw only two groups of pupils a day and stayed with them for two years; the schedule was simple and flexible, the curriculum inter-disciplinary.
- In 1995 a unique collaboration between school leaders, teacher unions, and the State Board of Education in Boston set up 'Pilot Schools' as laboratories for innovation and research, and development sites for effective urban secondary schools.
- The Pilot Schools have four essential features in common: high levels of autonomy and of accountability, a 'human scale' size, and a commitment to equality.
- Human scale is considered essential but not sufficient – it is what being human scale enables schools to do in the areas of pedagogy, curriculum, and assessment that really matters.
- Human scale puts relationships at the heart of school organisation and design. Staff teach 75 rather than over 250 students each week; each week students (to the age of 14) are taught by only four members of staff. Teachers know their students well and can create nurturing environments where young people are challenged to learn and behave to the highest standards.
- Human scale schools are 'thoughtful schools' with a reflective ethos; the staff is a professional learning community, thinking, planning and collaborating together.
- Human Scale schools offer young people a constructive experience of living in community, developing behaviours that are essential for their participation as citizens in a democratic and civil society.
- In 1994 in Denmark the Folkeskole Act promoted the design of a 12-year comprehensive school experience for all children with a commitment to: a socially relevant curriculum; interdisciplinary approaches to learning; the abolition of setting; education as an enterprise linking home and school; and school accountability to the local community.

- From the age of 6–16 students stay in the same school, with the same form teacher throughout and in the same class group until they are 15. Schools have a two-form entry system and no more than 500 students in total. Assessment is continuous and formative.
- From the age of 14, students can opt to spend a year in an Efterskole, a boarding school which usually has a particular focus, e.g. sports, music, the environment.
- Provision after 16 is varied and socially and educationally inclusive. It offers all students choices that meet their needs, are well resourced and have status.
- Does size make a difference? Recent evaluation of the Boston Pilot Schools showed improved outcomes in attendance, numbers of applications, exclusion rates, academic tests and graduation rates compared to other Boston state schools.
- The Pilot Schools have not proved more expensive – especially when the costs of social exclusion are calculated – and in some cases the schools have grouped together to share facilities and resources.

CHAPTER FOUR
Learning from the factors that make for a successful childhood

'Children who show persistent behavioural difficulties are often very troubled, with longstanding anxieties that relate to poor attachment and bonding in infancy ... and we need to look at new approaches to promoting resilience...'

Al Aynsley-Green, *The Guardian* (2006)[54]

Can we distil what we know about the securing of a successful childhood and apply this understanding to the design and organisation of our secondary schools so that all young people can engage positively with their schooling? What might our schools look like, how might they behave, if we were to use a model based in attachment theory? What can we learn from therapeutic practice in educational settings where organisation and design is already based in attachment theory?

Bowlby's model of attachment

John Bowlby's theory of attachment was first developed in the 1950s. The theory proposes that, unless children experience a secure relationship with an adult caregiver very early in life, they will struggle to develop normal social and emotional responses. Bowlby defined attachment behaviour as a 'biological instinct' which creates a need for children to be close to an 'attachment figure' when they feel anxiety about a possible threat. The expectation of the child is that the attachment figure will address and resolve the threat. The attachment figure provides a 'secure base in relationships' from which a child can explore the world, and a safe place to which a child can return.

Bowlby identified what he called 'internal working models', mental representations of the child and his/her human environment formed on the basis of early attachment experiences. These experiences shape a child's response to feelings of anxiety and security and affect his/her capacity to trust, to be open to learning, to contain anxiety, and to regulate emotions. Cognitive capacity may also be significantly affected by less than secure attachment.

If we argue that the development of these capacities is one of the key outcomes for a successful childhood, how can we use the intelligence gained from attachment theory to improve the design and organisation of our schools? Is it possible that, like 'attachment figures', our schools could provide 'a secure base in relationships' from which children could explore the world and a safe place to which they could return? A number of writers have begun to consider the implications of attachment theory when applied to learning in school settings.

A secure base and the 'learning triangle'

Educational psychotherapist Heather Geddes argues that attachment theory might help us to construct a model of schooling as a 'secure base' in which young people can work effectively – emotionally and cognitively – in a setting which offers them safety, security and stability. She is convinced that size matters and that 'in the small, more intimate community of primary schools, individual difficulties are more easily noticed and prioritised' and that 'there is more possibility of intervention at the inter-personal level and for integration of early intervention programmes into the policy and practices of the school.'[55]

She describes what she calls the 'learning triangle', which involves the presence of the teacher, the needs of the child, and the demands of the learning task, and she looks at how this can be used to address the different categories of attachment difficulties that children may face.

I believe that Geddes's work contains a number of ideas that should shape the training and professional development of all teachers. She explores not only the general principle of the learning triangle but looks in detail at how the presence of the teacher, the needs of the child, and the demands of the learning task can leave children with a sense of achievement, agency, enhanced resilience and a positive engagement with learning. She explores this model not only for securely attached children, but also for children who have insecure attachment styles. This is not the current language of one-year teacher training courses or ongoing professional development in our secondary schools, yet it needs to be if we are going to be able to re-engage disaffected young people within our schooling system. Awareness of the behaviours and responses associated with insecure attachment would help us as teachers to be sensitive to young people's anxieties in the face of challenges evoked by learning and school environments.

The school as 'containing parent'

Biddy Youell is a consultant child and adolescent psychotherapist at the Tavistock Clinic in London and Head of Training at the Northern School of Child and Adolescent Psychotherapy. In *The Learning Relationship: Psychoanalytic thinking in education,* she asks: 'What makes children want to learn in the first place?' and argues that as the mother provides the infant with a relationship that works well – or well enough – so the baby begins to take in an experience of 'being thought about' as a basis for the development of the capacity to think.[56] These very early sustaining relationships inform resilience and create attachment, a strong sense of identity and self-esteem. By contrast, an absence of this experience of 'containment', of 'being thought about' creates an infant who may be vulnerable to feelings of 'primitive anxiety'. Primitive anxiety overwhelms. Yet anxiety is important, as Youell points out, there is 'an inevitable anxiety and envy involved in learning'.[57] When a child enters formal education the school needs to understand its role as the 'containing parent' – containing the anxiety and ensuring that it does not get 'out of hand'. The challenge for teachers is how they 'can harness anxiety in the interest of learning and creativity'.[58]

Youell's analysis emphasises the importance of learning from experience, and of the child being accompanied by a 'strongly attached other' in the task of learning. She notes that children whose early experience is of not having been 'held in mind' grow up feeling that people do not like them. They are overcome by feeling states that they are unable to process without a great deal of help and they erect defensive structures to protect themselves. These structures, Youell argues, protect them from anxiety but make learning very difficult.

So what can teachers and schools do to work with those children who present with 'initial deprivation'? Youell suggests that this is an issue not only for individual teachers but for the whole way that a school as an organisational system functions. Schools must demonstrate their capacity for learning. Staff too must be 'held in mind' and have available the structures and systems, the times and places to enable them to talk to each other and take seriously the issues raised by their pupils.

Attachment theory could provide tools for education as well as for health professionals in the design of provision for young people. The ideal teacher-pupil interaction could be modelled on an early secure parent-child relationship, providing the young person with an experience of sensitivity, responsiveness, consistency and recognition, and act as a 'containment' for anxiety and distress. In this way, adolescents may develop a more integrated sense of self with the associated ability to regulate their emotions and adopt a more adaptive view of themselves and others. In this model, the school setting and the relationship environment it offers act as a 'quality care giver'.[59]

The programme 'Emotional Factors in Learning and Teaching: Counselling Aspects in Education' has been developed by Biddy Youell and her colleagues at the Tavistock Clinic and has been running for 30 years. Essentially it is making psychoanalytic ideas available in non-clinical settings. And whilst recognising that teachers are not therapists, Youell does draw attention to the 'therapeutic potential' of the relationships between teachers and pupils.

Secure attachment aids disposition towards learning

L. Alan Sroufe, Professor of Child Development at the University of Wisconsin, has highlighted that there are links between attachment experience and children's disposition towards learning, and that children who have experience of secure maternal attachment are 'involved with their teachers'. Children with a history of

> 'anxious attachment are less ego resilient and are more dependent, show more negative affect and negative behavioural signs, show less positive affective engagement with others and are less popular with their peers. In general they are emotionally less healthy than children with a history of secure attachment.'[60]

But securely attached children represent only 55 to 65 per cent of children in our schools; the rest struggle with the settings we have designed for them to learn in.[61] For children who have been emotionally and physically neglected or abused, even to begin to trust another adult is a huge task. These children may be hyper-vigilant to threat and remain in a persistent stress response.

This makes some school settings where these children face excessive demands difficult to bear let alone learn in. It also makes the demands on teachers seem overwhelming.

Behaviour is a communication about need

Teachers need a deep understanding that challenging behaviour is a communication about need. Youell suggests that pupils' rage may represent a primitive anxiety about survival in the face of almost constant threats and should be seen as defensive and protective behaviour; that separation and loss in a child's life can lead to a fear of their own destruction, and to panic. This view might enable a more informed professional response, but it is a very challenging perspective for teachers to accept, faced as they are with demands that exceed their resources and often their training, and in settings which may exacerbate rather than support their chances of responding appropriately.

Youell explores this dilemma:

> 'Teachers who face classes of 20 to 35 children, hour after hour, day after day, often protest that the kind of understanding offered in this volume is all very interesting but is of limited use to them. Their working lives, they say, are such that there is absolutely no room for anything extra. How can they possibly attend to the needs of every single child? How can they be expected to attend to the children's emotional development as well as delivering the National Curriculum, completing all the paperwork, and reaching their targets? A split opens up between those who are preoccupied with having to manage behaviour and those who seek to understand the child.'[62]

Indeed, as Youell acknowledges, many teachers cannot afford to open themselves up to children's emotional experiences or the reality of their home lives for fear of being overwhelmed. She suggests this may be why so many interventions in schools follow a strictly behavioural line, setting targets and relying on tariffs of rewards and sanctions.

Applying attachment theory

Substantial changes are essential if we are to create settings where teachers are able to attend to the level of need that Youell identifies. We must give teachers the working conditions, the structures, a manageable number of young people to relate to, the time for reflection, and the quality supervision that they require in order to promote young people's emotional engagement with learning. We must also enter into conversation with training providers. At present, I would argue that teacher training at secondary level is subject-focused with little emphasis placed on learning about child and adolescent development. The regulatory framework for training will need substantive review and reform to apply attachment theory properly to the way schools are organised.

We should seek to offer an experience of schooling which develops in young people a capacity to tolerate frustration and uncertainty, to have a sense of self as worthy of respect and affection, to develop empathy and the capacity to relate to others with respect, and which gives them a sense of personal agency – that young people are contributors to their life circumstances, not just products of them.

Educational practice in therapeutic communities

We can also learn from the application of attachment theory to the design and organisation of educational settings in therapeutic communities. These are communities where people suffering from long-term personality disorders, illness, and/or addiction live in community with the therapists treating them. Alan Worthington was the first Director of Thornby Hall, a therapeutic community and special school for children and adolescents. Reflecting on relationships and therapeutic settings he writes:

> 'These experiences need to be engaged with by the adults in a way that addresses their complexity, contains both adult and child anxiety, makes the development of dialogue possible, and establishes appropriate boundaries.'[63]

Worthington points out that while children in therapeutic communities have exceptional histories, what is true for these children, to a degree, is also true for a significant minority of children in mainstream secondary schools whose early attachment whilst not totally disabling has been substantially less than secure.

What might we usefully learn from therapeutic communities? Here we explore eight features of therapeutic communities in educational settings.

- How explicit theoretical frameworks inform policy and practice
- The concept of the 'holding environment'
- Providing a 'secure base' in relationships
- Characteristic approaches to behaviour management
- The role of key workers/attached adults
- The importance of leadership in containing anxiety
- The high profile given to staff development, training and professional supervision
- Working at a 'whole community' level

Explicit theoretical frameworks

In educational therapeutic communities, policy and practice are informed by an explicit theoretical framework. The development of the Urban Village School model – further discussed in the following chapters – is informed by the work of John Bowlby and fellow British psychoanalyst Donald Woods Winnicott; in particular by ideas around attachment theory and the holding environment. I believe this offers a much more relevant theoretical base than that used in many of our secondary schools. Some might suggest that there is no clear theoretical framework informing current policy and practice in our secondary schools, there is some loose commitment to 'ethos', variously inter-preted across a staff group. Where the theoretical framework is more explicit it does not usually go beyond behavioural or cognitive principles. I would argue that applying attachment theory as a clear theoretical framework, to inform schools' policies and practice, influence staff training, underpin approaches to behaviour, assessment, and relationships, and to which all staff were committed, would have a profound impact on the quality of secondary school provision.

The 'holding environment'

The concept of the 'holding environment', which is based on Winnicott's early work, shapes the design and organisation of thera-peutic community settings. It involves establishing a community which is based on understanding and tolerance, which has firm boundaries, and which emphasises the importance of communication in relation-ships. A 'holding environment' allows children to feel genuinely cared for, acts as a containment for their anxiety, promotes thoughtful res-ponses to events as they arise and a commitment to a personal and involved style of working. Crucially, it offers the stability and security essential for young people to begin to develop a sense of self and identity, the ability to relate to others and grow into mature and responsible adults.

There are implications in this model of working for the com-munity's style of leadership. A key task for the headteacher is to provide a holding environment for the staff – not only, I would suggest, so that staff can attend to their primary task of teaching, but also so that they can experience for themselves what it is they need to provide for their pupils. The quality of the holding environment for the staff in therapeutic communities is created mainly through the processes adopted by the management – in particular the use of a systems-based approach where it is recognised that all staff are dynamically linked and what affects one person affects all.

Providing a 'secure base' in relationships

Therapeutic communities recognise the need for creating a 'secure base' in relationships that might compensate for children's difficult past histories. Alan Worthington, now Director of the Peper Harow Foundation, notes that:

> 'These relationships are inevitably complex and these complexities need to be engaged with, thought about, understood, worked with in a contained framework that looks after the individuals involved.'[64]

This way of working – within a 'contained framework' – is addressed in therapeutic communities by establishing for each child a network of relationships that will hold and contain, protect, and provide opportunities for personal development. However the experience of many children in mainstream schools is one of insecurity and constant anxiety, with the breaks and transitions around school routines, timetables and programmes; the use of supply teachers; the numbers of relationships that children have to sustain each day and each week; the change of teachers each year and during the year; the insufficient resource and inadequate profile of tutors; the lack of regular shared rituals; and teachers viewed first and foremost as professional subject experts. All these factors and more mitigate against the establishment of a secure base in relationships and exacerbate the difficulties of less resilient children, those who have had less than secure attachment experiences.

If a fundamental premise of the development of the model of Urban Village Schooling is to design a setting where children learn in and through relationships, then providing opportunities for young people to *make* relationships becomes an explicit task, not an incidental outcome, of delivering a curriculum programme to a class. The role of mainstream schools should not be simply about the curriculum and the standards agenda, but also about developing a psychosocial model which integrates care, emotional development and education.

Approaches to behaviour management

What might the approach to managing difficult behaviour look like in a therapeutic setting? Clearly there is no universal model, but Adrian Ward, Senior Lecturer at the School of Social Work and Psychosocial Studies at the University of East Anglia, develops the idea of 'opportunity-led' work where the management of behaviour is in ways which can use 'opportunities for communication which arise out of daily interactions'.[65]

I would argue that teachers, products of the current training regimes, and schools, locked into current behaviour management systems, do not see challenging behaviour as important information about a child's need, or a prompt to reconsider the appropriateness of structures, systems and processes which govern young people's lives at school. Below I summarise the kind of scenario Ward creates to illustrate opportunity-led work, though he does acknowledge that in the 'busyness' of a school day teachers might not always find it straightforward to take such approaches.

In therapeutic communities, guidance about behaviour is clear and specific and arises from close consultation with staff.

- It begins with the need for detailed observation of any incident. What is happening? Who is involved? What is likely to happen next? How should I respond?
- From this detail further questions are asked. Is this an isolated incident? What are the current concerns and needs of the individual(s) involved? How may these be influencing events?
- The teacher is then asked to consider deeper questions about the incident. Why this person? Why this group? Why now? Has this happened before at this time, on this day of the week, at this time of year? And what is my instinctive response to this situation and what do my own feelings in this situation tell me about the behaviour and needs of those involved?
- Then decisions are taken in relation to the incident, setting out actions and a review, and managing closure.

All this requires attentiveness, responsiveness and creativity. It is a long way from the 'this is what you have done, and this is the penalty you will pay' style of behaviour management. It is about understanding challenging behaviour as a form of communication which, whilst needing appropriate boundaries, is also important information for teachers about a child's needs. The current design of our secondary schools makes this approach impossible in almost all cases. The challenge therefore is to design a setting where this becomes possible. We need to work at understanding the meanings underlying behaviour rather than seeking to screen out the difficult and disaffected, those who might affect performance targets and school league tables.

The role of the key worker or attached adult

A 'key worker' or 'attached adult' is someone who, as part of a network of relationships, provides a consistent and secure base for a young person throughout their secondary schooling. What characterises this role in therapeutic communities and what skill sets do the key worker or attached adult need?

A fundamental requirement for key workers is to be available in ways that are unthreatening. They might conceive their role as that of 'concerned adults', part of a 'transitional family' 'holding that child in mind' – a useful phrase to describe the consistent and reliable behaviour of the key worker. (It is the practice in foster care to provide 'transitional families', comprised of relevant professionals who meet regularly to 'hold the child in mind' and provide continuity between a child's past and future families.) The key worker does not see each challenging act as a separate incident to be 'handled', but part of a pattern of change moving the young person from where they are to where they want to be. But to be able to behave in this way requires that teachers have the time and expertise to do so, in well-designed and supportive settings where they can listen 'deeply'. It requires someone who can hold in mind everything about a child, his or her needs, helping them to find a way of talking about the things that matter. It is a day-to-day 'holding in mind', being available in a supportive way for some part of each day, especially when the child has an event or meeting that has a particular meaning, like an anniversary or significant transition, or is facing a threat. The key worker is the adult who is unconditionally there for the young person.

The challenge for the Urban Village School is to identify how to resource such a role within current budgets. However, if we are to provide a secure base, a key network of relationships, and contain anxiety so that the young person can trust enough to engage with learning, then this becomes a priority. This person is a key provider of the security, reliability and consistency that a significant number of young people yearn for when moving from primary to secondary school. This is more than the role of a Learning Mentor or even the Klasslaerer in the Danish Folkeskole, important though these roles are – it is an educational attachment role.

The role of leadership in containing anxiety

The distinguished psychoanalyst and social scientist Isabel Menzies Lyth stressed the connection between the task of the organisation and the anxieties which the task may generate in staff. She sets out how these anxieties influence the whole operation and how easily staff pool their anxieties into a 'collective defence', which inhibits the work that needs to be done.[66]

A central task facing mainstream secondary schools is to manage the transition from early childhood to young adulthood. There are many transitional phases during childhood and adolescence that create anxiety. Psychosocial theories proposed during the 1960s by German-born developmental psychologist Erik Erikson suggest a series of eight stages that extend from birth through to old age (infancy, early childhood, play age, school age, adolescence, young adulthood, adulthood and mature age) and in each of these he identifies internal personal conflicts to resolve before making a successful transition to the next stage, such as that between *trust* and *mistrust* in early childhood.[67] Such personal conflicts that *must* be successfully resolved – for example to have a successful childhood – create anxiety which cannot be allowed to run unbounded.

Important features of practice in therapeutic communities that contain and manage anxiety are the appropriate supervision of staff, consultation between staff, and their development and training. Amongst the headteachers of mainstream schools, the expression and understanding of the need to 'contain anxiety' to promote the primary task of the school is uncommon; as is also, I sense, the combination of supervision and consultation in the way therapeutic communities would understand these terms.

High profile for staff training and development

A major requirement for teachers working in communities under-pinned by explicit theoretical frameworks is that their training as teachers and their continuing professional development give them sufficient grounding to grasp the theory and the research, and the way these link to practice.

In therapeutic settings training needs to include psychodynamic and systems thinking, and attachment theory, as well as knowledge of recent relevant research in neuroscience. It is difficult to see how teachers can address the needs of troubled and disaffected young people without understanding what is happening to them in the exchanges and confrontations that are a common experience of a secondary school teacher handling a 'caseload' of over 200 young people a week.

Developing the skills and behaviours to be practitioners with an understanding of these theoretical frameworks needs to be an integral part of teacher training. In addition to training and staff development, ongoing consultation between and supervision for staff is essential. Debbie Meier, whose work was discussed in Chapter Three, argues strongly for schools which have time to think, where teachers have time to consult with each other, and where collaboration between the adults becomes a defining style of the school.

Sustaining the work within a therapeutic community is highly challenging for individuals. Supportive management of staff is an essential feature, allowing them to reflect on what they bring to their work, how they behave in their role, the way that the work and the institutional setting impacts on them, and how they impact on it and each other.

Working at a whole community level

Finally in this chapter let me detail a key and striking feature of therapeutic communities – the explicit commitment to working at a 'whole community' level. This sees all members of the community, adults and young people, contributing to each other's growth and development. It conceives of the community as a whole greater than its parts, where practice is conducted through a system of regular and frequent community meetings. The task for therapeutic communities is that of creating a single culture of understanding and seeing the members and experience of the community as a resource for the whole group.

Systems thinking, based on the work of psychoanalysts Eric Miller and Isabel Menzies Lyth, is central to working at a whole community level.[68] According to systems thinking, there is an 'inter-connect-edness' between the school community, the staff team, the student group, and the family group of any given child. This requires staff to hold all parts of the system in mind when addressing an issue or contemplating changes.

There is a particular phenomenon in therapeutic communities called the 'Large Group Meeting' or 'Community Meeting'. This might sound like a school assembly, but the function of the Community Meeting is significantly different. Alan Worthington describes the role of the Large Meeting which he developed at Thornby Hall:

'A large group meeting of this kind in a therapeutic setting is complex and works at a number of different levels, serving different functions. In general, it is a place where everything that impacts upon the group is acknowledged ... the essential element of this seemed always to me that staff could reassure the children's group, in whatever way, that they were mindful of and quite able to contain their anxieties and manage the issues that were driving it.'[69]

This is at the very heart of providing young people with an experience of living in community, and today schools may be the very last place, perhaps the only place, where such an experience is available for young people to take into their adult lives.

Of course, the opportunity for reflection might also be contained in other practices such as family group conferences, restorative justice approaches, and staff meetings at the end of each day to piece together an understanding of the day's events.

The challenges ahead

Incorporating these eight features into the model for an Urban Village School has very significant implications, but they are critical to the new school design and organisation that I will advocate in Chapter Five. These features cannot be incorporated without radically rethinking the training of our teachers and their ongoing continuing professional development, the role of university schools of education, the links between education and child mental health services, and the ways in which we can use research to build new knowledge for the future design of our schools.

Alan Worthington, whose writing on relationships in therapeutic settings we met earlier, highlights the tensions that exist within the present system. Our schools are having to face increased levels of need and expectation: the demand for clearer professional boundaries is welcome yet it leads to greater emotional distance from children; the demand for more scrutiny and regulation can result in more defensive practice; the emphasis on the individual is important but may lead to a lack of focus on the potential and importance of the group as a resource for its members. To what extent have education policy makers responded to very challenging issues – some of which I explored in Chapter One – with a battery of short-term initiatives rather than an analysis of the system as a whole?

All through this discussion I have been at pains not to blame those who are trying so hard to find powerful ways to work with young people, but rather to highlight the demands on teachers and schools for which they are insufficiently resourced. We need to emphasise the professionalism of our teachers and provide sufficient training and support. We need to create school settings where members of staff feel they are 'able to cope'. In practical terms we need to give teachers agency; we need to give them settings which support them in establishing relationships in depth that can be sustained over time, and significant space in the working week for collaborative practice, training and supervision. To make this possible does not require many minor amendments to current school practice but demands a major change to the design and organisation of our schools.

In the next chapter I further develop the idea of a different model of secondary schooling. These are human scale schools founded on the importance of building, maintaining and developing close, supportive and important relationships. I call these 'Urban Village Schools'.

Summary

- What factors make for a successful childhood? What implications do these have for the design and organisation of secondary schools?
- John Bowlby's theory of attachment suggests that children need a reliable 'attachment figure' and a 'secure base in relationships' in order to be able to trust, contain anxiety, regulate emotions and be open to learning – some of the key outcomes for a successful childhood.
- If the theory of attachment is used to inform the design and organisation of schools, then:
  - schools should be a 'secure base', in which young people can work effectively and which offers them security and stability;
  - school should act as a 'containing parent', with the teacher-pupil relationship modelled on an early secure parent-child relationship, providing young people with the experience of sensitivity, responsiveness, consistency and recognition that many lack at home;
  - teachers should understand the link between attachment and disposition towards learning (insecurely attached young people may be so anxious or hyper-vigilant to threat that they are unable to learn); and
  - schools need to understand that challenging behaviour is a communication about need.

- Up to 30 per cent of young people have attachment difficulties that are exacerbated by the current organisation and design of our schools.
- We can learn from the design and organisation of educational settings in therapeutic communities, which are influenced by attachment theory.
  - Policy and practice are informed by an explicit theoretical framework.
  - The community is a 'holding environment', based on under-standing and toleration but with firm boundaries, providing containment for anxiety for children and staff.
  - A network of relationships provides each child with a 'secure base' in relationships to try to compensate for difficult past histories.
  - Staff interpret behaviour as a communication about need and respond to it with attention and creativity.
  - 'Key workers' or 'attached adults' provide each child with a supportive adult who is consistent, unthreatening and uncondi-tionally 'there' for the child.
  - The leadership plays a key role in containing anxiety.
  - A high profile is given to staff development, training, consul-tation and supervision in order for staff to deal adequately with the demands they face.
  - Therapeutic communities work at a 'whole community' level, which is informed by systems thinking and sees all members, adults and young people, as contributing to each other's growth and development. A regular 'Community Meeting' allows every-one to meet together and discuss the issues that affect them.
- Using the theory of attachment to inform the design and organi-sation of mainstream schools will demand a paradigm shift in the way we train new teachers and provide ongoing supervision and continuing professional development; training should include developmental psychology, attachment theory, and psychodynamic and systems thinking.

CHAPTER FIVE
A proposed model for the Urban Village School

'The government should announce the end to the monolithic
secondary school. All children should be taught in schools (or
schools within schools) with no more than 500 pupils, where
they can form sustainable relationships with teachers, support
staff and peers.'

Charles Leadbeater, New Statesman (2008)[70]

The proposed model of an Urban Village School detailed here is an
exemplar, an encouragement for us to exploit the advantages of
human scale – small size being essential but not sufficient to set up
the kinds of schools where all young people can flourish. It seeks to
challenge the existing orthodoxy of large school communities and the
building of academies, which may in the end prove to be an expensive re-housing of our current difficulties with young people.

Let me stress very strongly at this point that this is not a prescriptive model but rather an illustration of how we might rethink the
design and organisation of our secondary schools. There is no sense
in which I am arguing that this is the only model that can be drawn
from the sources in the preceding chapters, but perhaps, as with the
Danish approach of designing provision to meet different needs, the
design principles I explore could be applied to a range of settings
or programmes.

The question to bear in mind throughout this chapter is whether,
as parents, this model provides the kind of setting that we would like
for our own children, or, as teachers, the kind of school organisation
and design in which we would be able to work and apply our professional energy and commitment.

In essence, my vision of an Urban Village School is of a learning
community where individual members of staff teach no more than 75
pupils a week, and relationships are placed at the heart of its organisation and design. The School will be co-educational and non-
selective, serving a designated community, with a total of 375 pupils,
aged 11–16. There will be a three-form entry structure, with 75 pupils
per year, and the year groups organised into three Halls, each with its

own community meeting room or Chapter House: the Foundation Hall (Years 7 and 8), the Senior Hall (Years 9 and 10) and the Graduation Hall (Year 11).

The model has ten distinguishing features:

1. A theoretical framework based in attachment theory
2. An emphasis on staff training and professional development
3. School size: a human scale learning community based on the importance of relationships
4. The structure of the school year
5. The timetable model
6. The teaching and learning approaches
7. The 'Learning Programme'
8. The 'Assessment Programme'
9. The 'Community Programme'
10. The concept of the school as a research community

Though the model I am proposing is not prescriptive, neither is it theoretical – this is a practical and coherent school model that could be built to replace the current provision of large secondary schools, and that would work in many areas of our inner cities where there is profound and widespread disengagement and disaffection. It might also be a feature of new housing communities, developed as urban villages on the edge of our cities to replace the large estates that have been so problematic since they were built in the 1950s. And could we not create, within existing housing estates, urban village settings with smaller Urban Village Schools serving these 'estate villages', where we could re-establish our connection with young people like Kirsten, Harry, Jacky and Devlin through human scale design?

What follows is an exploration of each of the ten distinguishing features of an Urban Village School. For each I provide a summary of its key conditions and a discussion of what the feature could mean in practice.

A theoretical framework based in attachment theory

- Attachment theory informs organisation and design
- Human scale settings
- Every young person has access to an 'attachment worker'
- Schools have a therapeutic disposition
- An emphasis on building emotional capital
- Resourcing teachers with the skills, understanding, and training to attend to the needs of young people

The theoretical framework that informs the organisation and design of the Urban Village School is explicit, shaping policy and practice within the school, and influenced strongly by attachment theory.

What will this look like in practice and what issues will it seek to address? Providing young people with access to adults with a working knowledge and commitment to the understandings that derive from attachment theory will create an environment where the importance of relationships is at the heart of the school's ethos and behaviour. This will be a school designed to support and resource a therapeutic disposition – where sensitivity, consistency and recognition are available to all its young people.

The human scale setting will allow teachers to be supported and resourced in time and in their training to provide a secure base in relationships for pupils coping with difficulties and anxiety. Anxiety is an unavoidable part of learning and development but so often in our schools it threatens to overwhelm some of our young people. In this Urban Village School model the school will act as a 'container for anxiety' to moderate stress, and soothe and support young people in regulating their emotions.

Each student will have access to an attachment worker to support their progress through school and make essential links with families. No student will work with more than four teachers a week, be in a learning group of more than 25, a year group of more than 75, or a Hall community of more than 150. The total school community when it meets together will be no more than 375 young people.

There will be a significant commitment to staff training and professional development in attachment theory supported by professional supervision. This will have implications for the priorities that the Urban Village School sets for itself, the way it allocates resources, and the ways in which the school is able to work as a community.

There should be an emphasis on the building of emotional capital – the set of emotional competencies which together represent the personal resource that each student needs for personal, social and economic success.[71] From the outset, our emotional competencies appear to receive less attention than physical and language development, and I would argue that this remains the case in much of our secondary schooling.

It is through these approaches and within these organisational settings that we will be able to move from using the language and behaviour of control to a language and behaviour that fosters the care and development of young people. In this setting young people will not feel a sense of isolation, they will not experience significant discontinuities, or be adversely affected by a lack of safe, reliable and consistent support from adult attachment figures. This will be a school resourced, organised and designed to provide its young people with opportunities to develop their emotional capital and with an experience of community that they can take into their adult lives.

An emphasis on staff training and development

- Training, supervision and consultation for all staff informed by developmental psychology and attachment theory
- Outreach training from providers like the Center for Collaborative Education (CCE) in Boston, USA, to inform pedagogy, curriculum design and assessment
- An international exchange programme linked to the Boston Pilot Schools Programme
- 20 per cent of every member of staff's week dedicated to training, professional development and supervision, and collaborative consultation and reflection
- Training on PGCE programmes to facilitate placements in Urban Village Schools

The implications and opportunities for staff in the Urban Village School are significant and call for a revolution in the way in which we train and support teachers working with challenging young people in our inner cities. In the Urban Village School teachers will be given the expertise and understanding to work professionally with young people who have high-level needs and who currently fall out of our school system with few qualifications and little stake in civil society.

Staff working within the Urban Village School will need to be committed to the theoretical framework that underpins its design and organisation, informed by developmental psychology, psychodynamic and systems thinking.

In the Urban Village School model, 20 per cent of a teacher's time in any week will be allocated to training, consultation and reflection, professional supervision and collaborative planning. This is a commitment to staff rather than a demand of them in the sense that it is saying that without this time and resource it is simply not reasonable to expect our teachers to respond professionally to the challenges they face.

There will be staff meetings at the end of each day to enable the staff to reflect together on those students who have found it difficult to engage positively in the learning programmes and to look collectively at ways of addressing their needs. Supervision from child psychotherapists and work discussion groups will be available to teachers and attachment workers to help them in reaching out to disaffected young people, and in understanding that challenging behaviour is often a communication about need and an acting out of remembered hurt.

In addition, prior to the start of each of the six terms, two-day residential meetings for all staff will provide time for them to anticipate the work ahead, think through the challenges they are facing, reconsider the design of their programmes, and concentrate on the complexity of their students and of the ideas with which they wish them to engage. The purpose will be to create a 'thoughtful school' as Debbie Meier describes it, where the professional and intellectual challenge is matched by an unconditional commitment to the students, their needs and success – an unrelenting commitment that, whatever it takes, no young person should fail.

Teachers will also be supported through involvement in a whole staff training and supervision programme similar to the Tavistock Clinic's 'Emotional Factors in Learning and Teaching – Counselling Aspects in Education' programme, which is now offered in partnership with the University of East London. Other programmes of professional development and support that could also be helpful are those offered by the Caspari Foundation, and the Nurture Group Network.

The approach to training provided by such organisations as the Tavistock would offer a coordinated programme enabling staff to reflect on the school's development and functioning with the support of psychoanalytically trained consultants. The programme would be a major investment in the professional development of the staff group, with a significant budget allocation each year.

Such a programme might include seminars covering psychoanalytic ideas and attachment theory, linked to the education context in which the staff is working. In addition consultation would be available for individual members to discuss in depth their interactions with troubled and troublesome pupils.

The training provision might also include the introduction of work discussion groups for staff teams in each Hall, providing a seminar setting led by a child and adolescent psychotherapist during which each member of the staff team would take it in turn to present a detailed written account of an interaction with a student, which would be considered by the group. In this provision the work discussion groups would meet throughout the year.

There would also be the opportunity for whole-staff training at the pre-term residential meetings which might for instance focus on topics such as 'Working with parents and families', 'Helping children and adolescents with social and behavioural difficulties' or 'Group dynamics at school'.

Training in new approaches to teaching and learning (pedagogy, curriculum design and assessment) is also central to this model of Urban Village Schooling and there would be an opportunity for it to be delivered initially through an outreach programme from, for example, the Center for Collaborative Education (CCE) in Boston. Linking staff in the Urban Village School to training abroad and professional development alongside teachers working in the Boston Pilot Schools would provide a wider base and greater motivation for learning.

The implications and opportunities for teacher training institutions, which might work in association with this model of Urban Village Schooling, are also significant. As the number of Urban Village Schools grows, there will be a need for a specific strand within the one-year Post Graduate Certificate of Education (PGCE) course for trainee teachers who wish to work in an Urban Village School. This could be negotiated locally and the programme might involve developing competences for interdisciplinary teaching and in the active inquiry, in-depth learning and performance assessment pedagogy, as well as providing training in developmental psychology, psychodynamic and systems thinking, and attachment theory. There would also be opportunities for teacher-training placements within an innovative Urban Village School, with a strong element of the programme based in research opportunities to provide commissioned research and training for the new role of 'attached worker'.

There needs to be a paradigm shift in the content, timing and delivery of our teacher training. The training of teachers needs a thorough overhaul and we should be looking at international models to review our provision. The four-year degree programme provided by Danish Seminariums might be one appropriate model to consider, as also the development of the role of 'social pedagogue' in Sweden.

School size: a human scale learning community

- Co-educational and non selective
- Serving a designated community
- Age range 11–16
- Three forms of entry
- School roll 375 pupils
- Year group of 75 pupils
- School structured into three Halls each with their own community meeting room (Chapter House): Foundation Hall (Years 7 and 8), Senior Hall (Years 9 and 10), Graduation Hall (Year 11)

This will be a school community designed on the scale of an urban village, where young people will learn in and through relationships and where every aspect of the school's design and organisation supports this.

The size of the Urban Village School community is linked to the need to promote autonomy, a sense of identity, manageability, agency and engagement. This is a school where staff will feel able to create a professional community committed to the needs of the children they teach. This is a school designed for all the children in a community. This is a school where children will be known and well known by staff and their peers, where they will be able to engage in learning and feel part not only of a small school of 375, but also of a smaller learning community of 150, and a year group of 75. This is a school designed to provide a secure base in relationships and a holding environment which will reduce the sense of threat and increase the level of trust. It is a place where the community will celebrate its successes and address its difficulties, where the group will be experienced as a resource for its members and where young people will gain an understanding of what it means to live in a community that fosters shared values which they can take into their adult lives.

It is a school whose primary task will be a focus on learning, a focus on each pupil achieving his or her academic potential, with an aspiration that its students will leave with affection for their schooling and a belief that they have a significant part to play as young adults in our society. In place of the anonymity and incoherence of the large secondary school, the Urban Village School will foster a powerful sense of community and a stronger commitment to academic rigour for all children.

The structure of the school year

- Six terms per year, each term lasting six weeks
- Two-week holidays between each term and four weeks at the end of the school year in the summer
- Two-day staff residential meetings prior to each term
- One day a week set aside for training, professional development and supervision, collaborative planning and reflection
- Eight-hour day from 10am to 6pm
- The working week organised around three programmes: the Learning Programme (three days), the Assessment Programme (one day) and the Community Programme (one day)

The design and organisation of the school year, the school term, and the working week is the framework for the provision of learning. The school year proposed here asks students to attend to their learning in six-week terms with a two-week break between each term and a slightly longer four-week break in the summer – concentrated periods of study linked with periods of relaxation, but not so long that there will not be a sense of continuity and application. The two-week breaks for students will also enable the staff group to meet in two-day residential retreats ahead of each term to reflect on the work of the school and the students' engagement.

The school day is eight hours, from 10am to 6pm. The late start partly acknowledges the research of Dr Kyla Wahlstrom and her colleagues at the Center for Applied Research and Educational Improvement at the University of Minnesota into the body rhythms of adolescents.[72] It also allows attachment workers to engage with families before the start of the day and to ensure that all students arrive on time. The later finish reflects the fact that all homework will be 'schoolwork', done in school time and supported by staff, and sends out a serious message of sustained engagement with young people. At the end of each day, the students will leave school knowing that they have done a good day's work, that this work is taken seriously by the staff, and that they do not have to take work home with them.

The design and organisation of the school week and school day is also informed by the view that we should keep organisational arrangements simple so that we can concentrate on the complexity of the young people and the complexity of the ideas they have to work with.

The working week is divided into three programmes, a Learning Programme, a Community Programme, and an Assessment Programme. The Learning Programme takes place over three days a week for each Hall, with the Community and Assessment Programmes taking up the other two days.

These programme arrangements enable staff and students to be clear about their focus for each day; and allow for maximum efficiency of teacher and attachment worker time and for 20 per cent of a teacher's time each week to be used for training, consultation, planning and supervision.

The timetable model

- Timetable directly managed by staff in each Hall
- Use of time tailored by staff to fit with Learning Programmes
- A flexible model of time use requiring no senior managerial input
- Traditional, extended, workshop and conference models available for teaching teams to choose from

The timetable will be designed to support the Learning Programme, providing teachers with direct control and agency over the way time is structured for learning. In each of the three Halls, a team of up to six teachers will have the responsibility of delivering interdisciplinary areas of study. This enables them to provide variety and, more importantly, to design schedules that are appropriate to the learning being undertaken, with the teaching and learning approaches that are most suitable for their age groups, their classes and the individuals within them. The Learning Programme for the Graduation Year (Year 11), for example, will be specifically and personally designed to meet the transition needs of each student, be it for progression to academic study in a Post-16 centre, vocational training at a college for further education, or through a diploma with a work-based programme.

The arrangements detailed here avoid the complexity and managerial costs associated with timetabling in large secondary schools, enable a 100 per cent room use at all times, and minimise the disruption resulting from student movement.

There are many possible ways in which staff teams within the Halls might structure the timetable for effective learning for their students. I offer some examples here. But it is important to remember that essentially this system gives teams of teachers the agency to decide what might work best – empowering them as a community of professionals.

- Traditional timetable: each of the three interdisciplinary areas of study has teaching and learning periods allocated to each class group as a traditional teaching period for each of the three days of the Learning Programme.
- Extended time model: the three days are used as half-day learning sessions, with two half days allocated to each interdisciplinary area of study.
- Workshop or field visit model: each of the three areas of study has a whole day allocated to run a Learning Programme or field visit.
- Conference model: each of the three interdisciplinary areas of study is allocated a three-day school-based or residential conference supported by the other teachers in the team.

Teaching and learning

- Active inquiry and research
- In-depth learning
- Performance assessment

The teaching and learning approaches proposed here are adapted from the model described by Tony Wagner, Co-Director of the Change Leadership Group at the Harvard Graduate School of Education, and formerly education adviser to the Bill and Melinda Gates Education Foundation.[73] They are in many respects similar to pedagogy adopted by the Coalition of Essential Schools in the USA, and supported by the Center for Collaborative Education (CCE) in Boston. They are based on three teaching and learning approaches which have significant implications for the way young people will learn and be assessed: active inquiry and research; in-depth learning, and performance assessment.

- Active inquiry and research: Students learn through participation, exploration and research; the activities they are set and engage in draw out perceptions and develop understandings. Students are expected to make decisions about their learning; and teachers to use the diverse experiences of the students to build effective learning.

- In-depth learning: This stresses depth rather than breadth in the curriculum coverage, with students required to struggle with complex and relevant problems, exploring core concepts of the interdisciplinary courses to develop deep understanding, and then to apply this knowledge in real world/local community contexts. This replicates a key feature of the Danish system – its emphasis on a 'socially relevant' curriculum.
- Performance assessment: Here clear expectations define what a student should know and be able to do. Students are required to produce quality work which is presented to real audiences. The work must show evidence of understanding, not just recall; and assignment tasks allow students to exhibit high-order thinking.

The approach to assignments and assessment, which carry a full day in the weekly programme, is discussed in detail later in this chapter, as is the make-up of the interdisciplinary curriculum. The timetable model I have outlined is an essential part of supporting these approaches to teaching and learning.

The Learning Programme

- Learning Programme is allocated three days each week
- Students' study is based on interdisciplinary courses
- Learning Programmes are delivered as a series of research assignments
- Core skills, concepts, competences and research habits are designed into these research assignments
- Teachers and pupils have a budget for 'expert witnesses' and 'residencies' to support the learning
- Each teaching team is supported by two teachers in training
- Attachment workers are linked to each Hall and support pupils with individual tuition and presentations for assessment. (Attachment workers also have 'all age advisory groups' which meet and work together in the Community Programme, which is detailed in the penultimate section of this chapter.)

The Learning Programme is allocated three days a week and is taught through interdisciplinary areas of study where common skills and knowledge are identified. Like the Royal Society of Arts (RSA) Opening Minds curriculum, the Learning Programme seeks to deal with competing curriculum demands.[74] It does so by:

- finding ways for specialists across the different disciplines to agree on skills and knowledge that are common to all;
- having a common approach to the 'habits of mind' and research methods that support learning;
- developing a curriculum that is informed by conversations with and is relevant to the community – local, regional, national and international;
- ensuring that the curriculum is not a mile wide and an inch deep in terms of the learning it offers;
- structuring the curriculum to ensure that students are learning in and through relationships where they are known and well known as learners; and
- focusing on key interdisciplinary areas of study.

With the introduction of Opening Minds, and programmes such as the Edison curriculum growing in popularity, an integrated approach (so widely adopted in primary schools) is being developed in many secondary schools here in the UK.[75]

The Learning Programme draws on the Enquiring Minds curriculum developed by Future Lab in Bristol, the arts-based approach at the Boston Arts Academy, and the use that the Fenway School in Boston makes of the concept of the city as a classroom.[76] Of course, different programmes have different emphases, but they share a number of themes.

1. Integrated curriculum approaches are based on core principles about the nature of learning.
2. They stress the importance of being as multidisciplinary as possible.
3. They adopt new approaches to assessment.
4. They foster links to the wider community.

The Urban Village School Learning Programme also emphasises active inquiry and research, in-depth learning, and performance assessment.

An example of how the curriculum could be delivered through interdisciplinary areas of study is given below. Again the emphasis on the collaborative approach from a professional community of teachers is important. Here I suggest four areas of study, with students taking three out of the four each term. A schedule showing this for the Foundation and Senior Halls is given on the following page.

- Science, technology, engineering and mathematics
- English, humanities and social studies
- The visual and performing arts
- Nutrition, fitness and health

This is an interdisciplinary curriculum not overly committed to competences but which seeks to engage young people in forms of knowledge, skills, education, and attitudes which will give them a higher status in society, termed cultural capital by Pierre Bourdieu and others – and develop a love of literature, of mathematics, of music, of scientific enquiry.[77] It contrasts strongly with the prevailing philosophy which is a 'predominantly functionalist and utilitarian model for state education (far removed from either the liberal model enshrined in much private education in Britain, or in the more radical models as captured in the Boston Schools.)'[78]

Each teaching team allocated to a Hall's Learning Programme has a devolved 'academic budget' to pay for 'expert witnesses': for example, a writer in residence, an artist, a nutritionist, an engineer or scientist. Students are involved with staff in identifying the support they feel they need for the research assignments they are working on. The Learning Programme requires staff who are able to teach within and across one of the interdisciplinary subject-based areas and this has implications for staff training. (In Denmark, there is an extended training programme where teachers of children up to the age of 14 learn to teach across at least three subject areas.)

A Learning Programme for the Foundation Hall or Senior Hall might be shaped as follows. The example given is for the Year 7 Learning Programme for one of the three classes in the Foundation Hall over a six-term year. Again, I emphasise that this is not prescriptive – what is being argued for here is a dynamic, reflective approach to curriculum design, to learning approaches, and to assessment.

Foundation Hall (Year 7 Programme)

Term 1
science/engineering/maths/
    technology
English/humanities/languages
visual and performing arts

Term 2
nutrition/fitness/health
science/engineering/maths/
    technology
English/humanities/languages

Term 3
visual and performing arts
nutrition/fitness/health
science/engineering/maths/
    technology

Term 4
English/humanities/languages
visual and performing arts
nutrition/fitness/health

Term 5
science/engineering/maths/
    technology
English/humanities/languages
visual and performing arts

Term 6
nutrition/fitness/health
science/engineering/maths/
    technology
English/humanities/languages

Each course would be based on a research assignment lasting six weeks and pupils would also have access to ten hours of individual tuition each term through the Assessment Programme to support their work. The research assignments would be designed to develop knowledge, core skills and 'habits of learning', and an understanding of key concepts, through issues of local, national and global relevance to the students.

A research assignment in the study area of science, technology, engineering and mathematics might look at 'investigating and designing responses to epidemics'. The students would learn to use mathematical models to explain the impact of epidemics on the world (swine flu or HIV for example). They would examine and model how different epidemics have spread. They would use models to predict patterns for current threats and design ways of responding to them. The research assignment would be clearly structured into weekly assessment tasks and all learning would be supported by specific inputs from teachers and expert witnesses, as well as by the individual tuition programme.

Extending the school day to 6 pm will provide essential additional study time for students to work on their weekly assessment tasks within school with all the facilities and support they may need. It is also the time when individually designed one-to-one tuition, catch up groups and extension programmes can be made available and when attachment workers can follow up issues with individual students and their families to support engagement and learning.

The Assessment Programme

- Assessment Programme allocated one day a week
- Assessment tasks are set each week linked to the learning research assignment in each of the interdisciplinary areas being studied
- Assessment is structured through group assessment reviews, performance assessment, and narrative reports

The Assessment Programme is allocated a full day each week and has three elements: weekly group assessment reviews; performance assessment; and yearly narrative reports.

Many of the ideas here are drawn from human scale practice in Boston and New York. In Boston there is an accommodation with the State Education Board to allow for performance assessment alongside state testing, and in New York the small school movement has negotiated a dispensation from standardised testing for a fixed period to allow for the development of performance assessment.

With the ending of Key Stage 3 National Curriculum testing, and the increasing agitation from school leaders, teacher unions and parents about over-testing in schools, new approaches to assessment such as the examples offered here become possible. In the Urban Village School, each Hall has its own Chapter House, providing a space where assessment activities can easily be accommodated.

The emphasis on reflective assessment is central to ensuring that all students reach their potential. On a weekly basis staff can gauge each young person's progress and concentrate on how as individuals and as a group the students in each Hall can develop their understanding and make the improvements that are necessary.

Weekly group assessment reviews

Structured and supported assessment tasks will be set in each interdisciplinary area for each pupil every week. These will be designed to be an element of the research assignment that the students are undertaking over the six-week term and will support their classroom-based learning programmes. As part of the Assessment Day Programme there will be a plenary at which group feedback will be given on the way the previous week's assessment task has been managed, highlighting areas that have been well done, where further thought is necessary, and where learning has been difficult. This approach emphasises the importance of the group's learning and how its engagement in the process of struggle and success in learning is seen as a resource for everyone. It will demonstrate what it means to be in a cooperative academic community where success for everyone is given the highest priority.

Performance assessment

Regular performance assessments allow pupils to demonstrate the knowledge, understanding and skills they have gained through their research assignments, as well as being the process through which they are awarded their grade and standard in each of the interdisciplinary areas of study at the end of each year. Supported by their attachment worker, each student makes a presentation to an audience made up of members of the Hall staff team, two invited student members from the students' 'all age advisory group', a member of their family group, and an external moderator from the linked university. The student is required both to present their work and to defend it. An attachment worker may act as a 'corporate parent' at the performance assessment, where family settings make this necessary, and this underlines the importance of the family being represented in valuing the learning of each student.

Narrative reports

Pupils have individual meetings with the Co-Directors (Headteachers) of the Urban Village School each term. Again, students are supported by their attachment workers at these meetings, which confirm their attendance, punctuality, progress, achievements, contributions as learners, as research associates, and as community ambassadors. These form the basis of a report awarded to each student at a graduation ceremony held in the school at the end of each year, which includes the academic standards that have been attained through their performance assessments. The graduation ceremony provides some of the ritual that is so often missing in our large schools – ritual which gives meaning and recognition to student achievement.

The Community Programme

- Community Programme allocated one day a week
- Key role for attachment workers in this programme
- Programme delivered through vertical age groupings which are 'advisory groups' with students drawn from across each of the three Halls (Foundation, Senior and Graduation)
- Health and Advice budgets are allocated for each pupil
- 60 hours of individual tuition a year allocated to each pupil
- Pupils have Chapter House meetings in their Hall three times a week, and Community Meetings as a whole school twice a week
- Each week the Community Programme provides opportunities for Leadership and Challenge activities, sporting events using local community facilities, whole school events, community service/ ambassador programmes, and internships in local companies
- Community Programme is supported by additional external resources and personnel

As explained earlier, each student has access to an attachment or key worker, an 'attached adult' who is there to support the student in whatever way is necessary – getting students to school, developing links with their families, addressing students' personal issues, guiding them at times of transition, arranging individual tuition, and helping them prepare for performance assessments.

Each attachment worker has a mixed-age caseload of pupils, an advisory group of 11–16 year olds (what is known in some schools as a family learning or support group) who are supported by the attachment worker through their school career. Attachment workers provide the emotional backbone to the students' school life and have the same status as teachers and the same access to staff development, training, consultation, and supervision from child psychotherapists. Along with the Co-Directors, they are responsible for the Community Programme.

In addition to the funding available for the Community Programme, the attachment worker has two budgets specifically allocated for their advisory group. The first is a Health and Advice Credit Allowance which, in discussion with students, can be used to support their particular needs in order to improve their engagement in learning. This might be providing access to a dietician if the pupil is overweight and concerned about this; it might for example be used to gain counselling support or fund an activity which will increase a young person's confidence and engagement.

The second is the Individual Tuition Budget which will provide up to 60 hours of individual tuition for each student a year. With input from student and teacher, the attachment worker is there to identify which specific areas of learning the student might need to concentrate on – be it basic skills in numeracy or literacy or additional programmes of extension or enrichment.

The attachment workers and the Co-Directors of the Urban Village School arrange and supervise the Community Programme, a programme of whole school events which takes place for one day each week, releasing the teaching teams for collaborative planning, consultation, training and supervision. The programme provides an opportunity for students to use their skills and aptitudes to make a contribution in the wider community beyond the school – developing a sense of mission for their community. The Community Programme is significantly funded to allow additional resources and skills and personnel to be engaged in identified programmes within the school and the wider community.

Opportunities within the day-a-week Community Programme might include community projects, workplace internships, sporting and musical events, challenge and leadership programmes or a school production. The programme is about developing the students as community ambassadors – making a contribution together in their local area and in the process gaining important leadership skills.

On three days a week there will be a Chapter House meeting for each Hall and twice a week the whole school will come together in a

Community Meeting. This is the time when the whole community offers itself as a resource for its members, celebrating its successes and reflecting on behaviour and difficulties. It is the place where the Urban Village School recognises itself as a community whose interests are supported by its members. The emphasis on working at a whole community level is drawn from ideas I presented in Chapter Four: applying psychodynamic and systems thinking to enable the whole school community to reflect on its behaviours and achievements, to contain anxiety and to celebrate success.

Throughout this book I have made the argument that schools have a role in promoting the interest of the community rather that allowing self interest to be young people's only motivation; that there is a danger that education may become like a market place in which young people develop their identity as consumers rather than as citizens. The features of the Urban Village School which emphasise Community Ambassadors and the Community Meeting are designed to counteract this and prevent young people from leaving our schools with little or no experience of community living which they can take into their young adult lives, and which will help them contribute to civil society.

The school as a research community

- Pupils and staff are research associates
- Teachers in training have a research focus
- The school itself commissions research into school organisation and design

The Urban Village School is also conceived as a 'Learning and Research Community' which provides information for the Urban Village School itself and importantly for the wider educational community. This has several dimensions.

Students and staff would be 'research associates' working, as part of their programme, on the study and critique of secondary school designs, nationally and internationally, and using this work to inform the development of their own educational setting. This role challenges students to be key players in the development of their school as a Learning and Research Community, working to build new knowledge about the design and organisation of schools alongside educational researchers and practitioners. The students would be asked to reflect on their own experience of schooling and interrogate different models of schooling within the UK and beyond. There are possibilities here to work collaboratively with other schools and agencies, for example the Boston Pilot Schools, the Center for Collaborative Education in Boston, the Julia Richman Educational Center in New York, and the Folkeskoles and Efterskoles in Denmark.

Links with a university school of education will enable trainee teachers to undertake action research alongside Urban Village School teachers as part of their placements in the school. The Urban Village School will provide a rich data set based on the narratives of the teachers and young people working in the school, and a key function will be to commission research on innovative practices, for example, on the effectiveness of the Learning Programme, on its supervision and assessment methods, the role of the attachment worker, the use of child psychotherapists, or the role of the Chapter House or Community Meeting.

The Boston Pilot School leaders all made the point that whilst being human scale is essential it is not sufficient. It is what becomes possible in human scale settings that makes the difference – to learning, to assessment, to relationships, to the creation of communities of professionals able to shape and collaborate on their work with young people, to the whole school's sense of community. All of this begs the question: what would an Urban Village School look like? What settings might support the successful implementation of the proposals I have made. In the next chapter I work with architects to visualise the Urban Village School.

CHAPTER SIX
An architect's view

I have developed the concept of the Urban Village School as a human scale learning community in discussion with the Stirling Prize Award-winning architects practice, Feilden Clegg Bradley. In our early conversations it became clear that this project was very different from the designs for new schools which the architects had developed for the Building Schools for the Future (BSF) programme, for two reasons. The first was that we needed to respond to the question of the feasibility of scale; the second was that it provided the opportunity to consider *how* the explicit philosophy behind an Urban Village School could inform its design.

Is the Urban Village School model feasible?

It was clearly going to be essential to demonstrate that building a school, on a human scale with a maximum of 375 students, was both feasible and cost effective in terms of allowable space per student within government guidelines, as set out in Building Bulletin 98 (BB98), the briefing framework for state-funded secondary school building projects.

All through this work, when I have been giving presentations at conferences and in my discussions with a number of local authorities, I have been challenged to show how this human scale Urban Village School would meet the space constraints set down by BB98. During 'The Children Left Behind', I asked Peter Clegg at the Bath offices of Feilden Clegg Bradley whether this would be possible, whether it was feasible. His answer was clear: it was feasible, it was possible, and solutions were already emerging, for example, there were now 'schools within schools'.[79] In many American cities existing large high schools are being broken down into smaller learning communities, and this is a movement that is accelerating in the United Kingdom where for example, Brislington Enterprise College in Bristol has been reorganised into five small learning communities.[80]

Other 'solutions' are the design and organisation of the state-funded academy for the Steiner Foundation in Hereford, and in Wiltshire where the local authority is seeking to transform the educational outcomes in

Salisbury by building new academies on human scale principles. In Cumbria, seven small rural schools, which make up the Rural Academy of Cumbria, are successfully raising the attainment of their students, with three of the schools amongst the top five most improved schools in England in 2008. Most of the Rural Academy of Cumbria schools have less than 250 pupils and the largest has just over 600.

Initial plans

Initial work therefore was to set out and cost a schedule where the square metre allowance per student could be accommodated within the government guidelines. Figure 1 (opposite) illustrates the space requirements for the school. Note how, even at this stage, the plan includes a Chapter House for each Hall, for meetings, presentations, performance, learning reviews, social activity and dining, and how the Community Hall and Research Centre are at the heart of the school. In order to allow for the Chapter House, Community Hall and Research Centre, the allocation of facilities does not include specialist sports provision, though the Foundation and Senior Halls both have a nutrition/health/fitness studio catering for these within interdisciplinary areas of study. The philosophy behind the design is to concentrate on essential learning spaces and on facilities which will create a strong sense of community within the school. Where specialist facilities for sport or other activities are needed, these would be accessed in the wider local community as and when required – Fenway High School in Boston provides a good model of the school being part of the city community in this way.

In Figure 1 the schedule of accommodation comes close to meeting the Government BB98 guidelines. For a meaningful comparison with current secondary provision (where schools often have 1,000 or more pupils), three linked Urban Village Schools of this size would require 9,726 sqm in total compared to the allowance by BB98 of 9,388 sqm or an allowance per student of 8.6 sqm which only very marginally exceeds the 8.3 sqm set out by the guidelines BB98.

Three linked schools

The early discussions with the architects looked at ways in which the Urban Village School model might be an opportunity to create a number of linked schools, working collaboratively, each with a defined specialism. This could provide a schooling offer to a community for all its young people, and still benefit from the intimacy of human scale design.

Plan and sections

1:550

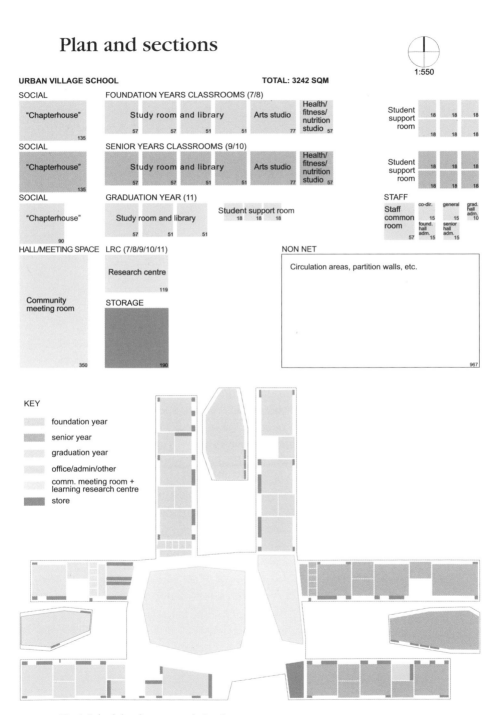

URBAN VILLAGE SCHOOL   **TOTAL: 3242 SQM**

SOCIAL   FOUNDATION YEARS CLASSROOMS (7/8)

"Chapterhouse"   Study room and library   Arts studio   Health/fitness/nutrition studio
                          57   57   51   51   77   57
135

SOCIAL   SENIOR YEARS CLASSROOMS (9/10)

"Chapterhouse"   Study room and library   Arts studio   Health/fitness/nutrition studio
                          57   57   51   51   77   57
135

SOCIAL   GRADUATION YEAR (11)

"Chapterhouse"   Study room and library   Student support room
                          57   51   51   18   18   18
90

HALL/MEETING SPACE   LRC (7/8/9/10/11)

                          Research centre
                          119
Community
meeting room   STORAGE

350   190

Student support room   18 18 18 / 18 18 18

Student support room   18 18 18 / 18 18 18

STAFF

Staff common room   co-dir. / general / grad. hall adm. 10 / found. hall adm. 15 / senior hall adm. 15
57   15   15

NON NET

Circulation areas, partition walls, etc.

967

KEY

- foundation year
- senior year
- graduation year
- office/admin/other
- comm. meeting room + learning research centre
- store

Fig. 1. Schedule of accommodation for
one Urban Village School

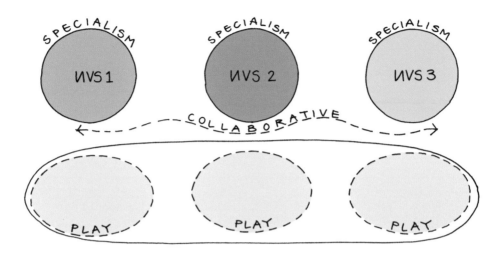

Fig. 2. Conceptual drawing for three
linked schools

Figure 2 (above) is a conceptual drawing of three Urban Village Schools configured to do just this. This could easily work with two, four or even five Urban Village Schools. Working collaboratively, the schools might combine to provide for an orchestra or competitive sports teams or share recreational facilities. They might also share programmes of study for the Graduation Year as students prepare for transition into Post 16 education or for diploma programmes.

Would this not be a better provision of secondary schooling for our large inner-city housing estates or for renewing those post-war housing developments on the edge of cities? Could it not provide planners who are developing concepts of urban villages within large estates the opportunity to create smaller communities with a sense of identity, each with its own Urban Village School, but working in close partnership with its neighbours? This model might work to support schools in Salisbury to develop as an academy whilst maintaining the smaller learning communities which are a key element of their current design as family-based faith schools. It is the model of the Rural Academy in Cumbria but in a more integrated setting.

Having time for philosophy to influence design

A major difference in the way in which this model of an Urban Village School was developed with the architects was that we were able to take our time. We were not working to a 12-week deadline from first discussion to outline design, and this was not a conversation about which 'off-the-peg' model the client wanted – 'pavilion', 'atrium' or 'street' – to meet the needs of a 1,100 student school. The architects had time to consider in depth the thinking behind the proposed Urban Village School.

Working with the internal intellectual architecture

This was an approach where the 'internal intellectual architecture' of the school – the organisational design informed by an explicit theoretical framework – was as important as the external design of the building. It was crucial that the architects were able to 'hold in mind' the ideas that were informing this model of schooling and to think deeply about how to create the settings and visualise the spaces that would enable a learning community based on the primacy of relationships.

The architects had also to hold in mind the voices of Kirsten and Harry, of Devlin and Jackie, their lack of recognition, their need to be known and well known. The designs had to address the sense of isolation that these young people and so many others experience in large secondary schools, and make available to them the safety, consistency and reliability which they had enjoyed at primary school.

The task for us all was to show how the theoretical framework might be reflected in the built environment. Feilden Clegg Bradley cited the Austrian educationalist Rudolf Steiner who argued that architects should make the 'whole building as if it possessed a soul'. Arguably, this is a little removed from the language and approach used in relation to a BSF or private finance initiative new build.

The plans for an Urban Village School were developed initially through early conceptual drawings in which we tried to find a way to express the importance of the key ideas and concepts – a 'secure base in relationships', a 'holding environment' where young people would be thought about and properly regarded, a school where attachment figures might be able to 'contain anxiety' and where young people would live and learn in a community that had depth and meaning.

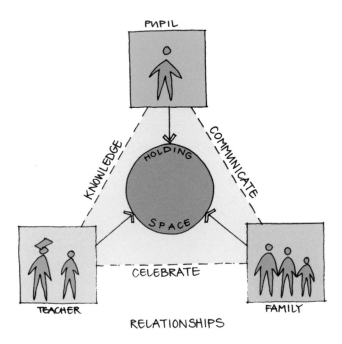

Fig. 3. The school provides a holding
space for pupils, families and staff

Putting relationships at the heart of the school

Our first attempt was to look at the importance of relationships within
a system where all the key participants, teachers, pupils and families,
could be represented. Figure 3 (above) shows how all three groups
would see the school as a 'holding space' to which they contributed
and from which they were resourced. It emphasises the importance
of roles, of the primary task of the school (teaching and learning), and
of boundaries and how the whole enterprise is underpinned by the
primacy of relationships – an acknowledgement that we all learn in
and through relationships. Here students learn from teachers, families
stay in touch with their children's learning, and teachers and families
celebrate student achievement. This communication and celebration
between staff, students and families would be embedded in practice
through the performance assessment and narrative reporting described
in Chapter Five and in the ritual associated with the transitions from
the Foundation Hall to the Senior Hall and on to the Graduation Hall.

Learning in community and the importance of staff training

Figure 4 (below) shows how the three Hall communities (Foundation, Senior and Graduation), each with their heart in their own Chapter House, form part of the whole school and come together in the Community Hall which sits at the very centre of the school. Here all 375 students would meet together to share success and reflect on the values that inform the policies and practice of the school. Figure 4 underlines the importance of giving students an experience of living and learning together in community which they can take into their adult lives.

It also emphasises how the training and support of the adults working in the school is of the utmost importance. The outer line of the diagram represents the input of external training from organisations like the Tavistock Institute in London, the Caspari Foundation or the Nurture Group Network, and linked academic partners in university schools of education. Furthermore, such links represent the importance in this model of provision for the professional development and supervision of staff. It emphasises that this is a school community where there is structured time for staff to consult with each other, time for collaborative planning and design, and for reflection, with 20 per cent of staff time dedicated to this and six two-day residential staff conferences each year.

Fig. 4. The three Hall communities come together in the Community Hall at the centre of the school

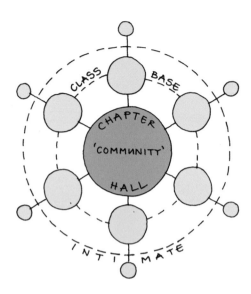

Fig. 5.Tiers of community and support
in an Urban Village School

Living and learning in a community

The discussion with the architects moved from the overall organisational design to examine what the Hall communities represented, how each Hall might provide for learning, and how pupils might be supported in this learning by attachment workers. Figure 5 (above) reflects some of this, although the introduction of the all age advisory groups (family learning groups) came at a later stage when it was clear that a way needed to be found to integrate students from the three Halls. The conceptual drawings were the start of the conversation and so do not capture all the features which appear in the detailed drawings discussed at the end of this chapter. It is important to mention this, as the iterative process of discussion, conceptual drawings and further discussion was integral to the development of the model and was only possible because we had sufficient time.

One of the most revealing remarks about small schools was made during the course of filming 'The Children Left Behind' when I asked an Afro-American student at Fenway High School in Boston what was so important about being a student in a school of just over 300 students. The immediate reply from the student was: 'There's a lot of love in a small school.'[81] What Figure 5 is beginning to express is how we create school communities that are intimate, where students are held in unconditional positive regard. It shows a Hall community for 150 students which, with its Chapter House, six class bases and six counselling spaces (for attachment workers), might provide a secure base in relationships where all students could thrive and learn. This is a setting where any previous experience of isolation and discontinuity would be strongly counteracted and where staff can concentrate on the complexity of the students and the complexity of the ideas the students will have to work with.

The Urban Village School as a research community

The final conceptual drawing (Figure 6, below) explores the idea of the Urban Village School as a research community with staff and students taking on an additional role as research associates, with their practices being reviewed and supported through action research programmes linked to academic partners.

The small circle within the Urban Village School, labelled LRC, is the Learning Research Centre. This is not only an essential resource for students undertaking research assignments as part of their inter-disciplinary areas of study, but also a base for the research partnership between the school and a linked university school of education.

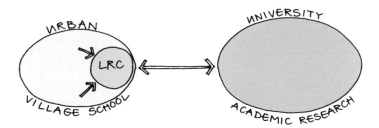

Fig. 6. The Urban Village School as a research community

Taking a walk through the Urban Village School

It was at this point that we began to look at how the schedule of accommodation, informed by the theoretical framework (captured in the conceptual drawings), might be configured. It is important to re-state that this is not a prescription for what an Urban Village School should look like, but an illustration which would change given different contexts. What is crucial though are the principles informing the design and organisation of the school – the way the ten features described in the previous chapter are expressed and facilitated by the detailed design of the built environment.

A number of organisational layouts of the accommodation were con-figured and considered. The decision was made to place the Community Meeting Room and the Research Centre at the heart of the building linking the Hall Communities on each side, as the most coherent way of expressing the philosophy behind the building. In other words that this is a school which builds community through relationships, where the learning model is through research assignments, and where all members of the school community are research associates building new knowledge about the design and organization of schools informed by human scale and attachment theory.

The human scale building envisaged by the architects emphasises the importance of the school being a learning *community*. This is close to the design of the Year 10 Klasseskole in Albertslund, Copenhagen, featured in Chapter Three, where the one-storey building creates a sense of calm, space, and belonging. The Community Meeting Room at the centre of the building and the Chapter Houses that serve each Hall Community have raised rooflines, giving them height and prominence. This stresses the importance of community and of giving young people a positive experience of living in community which they can take into their adult lives.

The facilities that are provided internally are shown in Figure 7. Students enter through the entrance court and garden (18) – a gathering place where staff and students can welcome each other at the start of the day and take their farewells at the end of the day. There is a reception desk (19) to the left, as they enter the school, which serves the whole community and in particular parents and visitors, although each Hall community also has its own administration base (20), which provides for closer care and communication with the students and their families within each of the Hall communities. Past the reception desk there is an entrance hall which leads off to each of the three Halls, the Foundation Hall for Years 7 and 8, the Senior Hall

Plan and sections

1:550

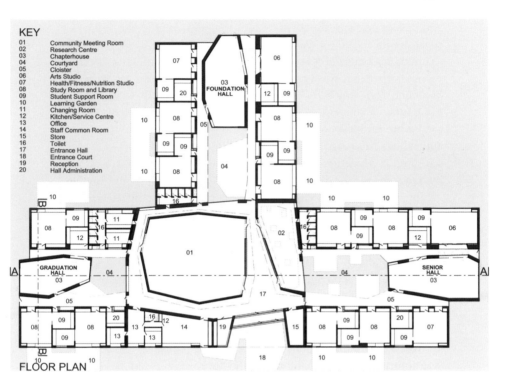

KEY

01 Community Meeting Room
02 Research Centre
03 Chapterhouse
04 Courtyard
05 Cloister
06 Arts Studio
07 Health/Fitness/Nutrition Studio
08 Study Room and Library
09 Student Support Room
10 Learning Garden
11 Changing Room
12 Kitchen/Service Centre
13 Office
14 Staff Common Room
15 Store
16 Toilet
17 Entrance Hall
18 Entrance Court
19 Reception
20 Hall Administration

FOUNDATION HALL
GRADUATION HALL
SENIOR HALL

FLOOR PLAN

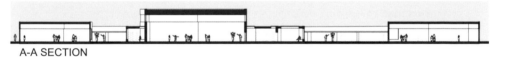

A-A SECTION

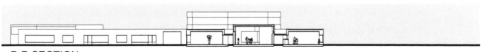

B-B SECTION

Fig. 7. Plan and sections showing the
facilities and layout of an Urban Village
School

for Years 9 and 10, and the Graduation Hall for Year 11. These are the three small learning communities within this Urban Village School.

To the left of the entrance hall is the Community Meeting Room (01). This is at the centre of the school and links directly to each Hall and has an entrance for access from each Hall community. This, in a sense, is the 'nave' of the school where the community gathers to share, to celebrate and to reflect, and it can be used as a large meeting room and performance space. It has an internal cloister surrounding it. Modelled on practice in therapeutic educational settings, the Community Meeting Room is the place where everything that impacts on the life of the school community is acknowledged and discussed, and where the primary task is that of creating a culture of understanding in which the members of the community are seen as a key human resource for the whole community.

The Community Meeting Room is also essential for the Community Programme, when for one day a week the three Halls will come together as a whole school community. The Community Programme will enable students working in groups drawn from all ages and across the three Halls to participate in leadership and challenge activities, sporting events, and community service and ambassador programmes – whole school initiatives and efforts which not only create a sense of community within the Urban Village School but see the Urban Village School making a distinct contribution to its local and wider community.

To the right of the entrance hall is the Research Centre (02). This is also at the heart of the building. In the same way that the Community Meeting Room represents the importance of the community dimension of the school, the position of the Research Centre emphasises the importance of learning, knowledge and research as a primary task of the school. It is also, as we have seen, a statement about the school's role as a research community linked to academic partners and training providers. Research centres are modelled on the Boston Pilot school design where the word 'Pilot' means a school committed to innovative practices in structure, processes, teaching, learning and assessment, and to sharing these new ideas openly with other schools, building new knowledge about the way education is offered and accessed.

The additional spaces around the Community Meeting Room are a store room (15) to service the equipment and furniture needs of the Community Meeting Room, a staff common room (14), offices for the Co-Directors and whole school administration (13), a kitchen area (12) and toilet facilities (16) for staff. Finally, off the internal cloister of the Community Meeting Room are two changing rooms (11) to provide facilities for students for, for example, drama and dance.

Zones

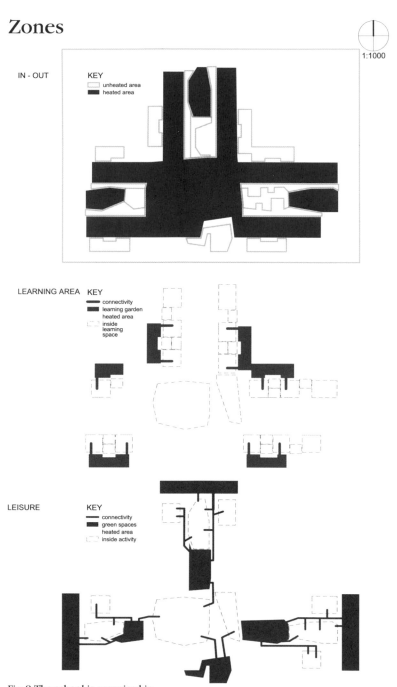

Fig. 8. The school is organised in
zones to maximise cost-effectiveness
and sustainability

In the Urban Village School it is possible to hold the whole building 'in mind'. Its human scale and its design create a sense of calm and manageability for all who live and work in the building and for those who visit.

The architects also considered environmental issues with regard to heating and the use of inside and outside spaces. The building is organised in zones, as can be seen in Figure 8 (previous page). This makes efficient use of resources. The principles of providing a well insulated building, maximising natural light with an efficient monitoring and evaluation system including zoned control are fundamental to the school design. Despite the large building envelope generated by the single storey scheme, the building benefits greatly from being able to maximise natural daylight and ventilation, and the opportunity for timber construction. The drawn scheme is based on a suburban site, where a generous site allows for optimum orientation, views, natural cross ventilation and excellent daylighting. Sustainability issues are addressed in the widest sense, from exemplar low energy passive design principles to circulating externally for healthy living and a healthy eating agenda supported by school allotments. With the UK government ambition for all new school buildings to be zero-carbon by 2016, there are significant challenges for the design, management and use of school buildings.

The Hall Communities

Finally we come to a detailed look at the Hall Communities, see Figure 9 (opposite). Each Hall is a distinct learning community with its own wing of the school and its own facilities. These facilities are built around a cloistered courtyard (leisure garden). Each Hall has four class bases, which here are described as study room and library, and two more practical workspaces/studios which provide for the interdisciplinary study areas for the arts and for nutrition, fitness and health. The study rooms have access to external learning gardens as well to the internal courtyard via the cloister.

In addition, each Hall has six student support rooms for small group work and for consultation with attachment workers who support students individually and through the all age advisory groups which serve to integrate students across the Halls.

The facilities for each Hall include an administrative office to support staff, students and families (a communication centre dealing with lateness, illness, absence and family contact as an integral part of the Hall community's function), a kitchen service area, and toilet

Detail drawing

1:300

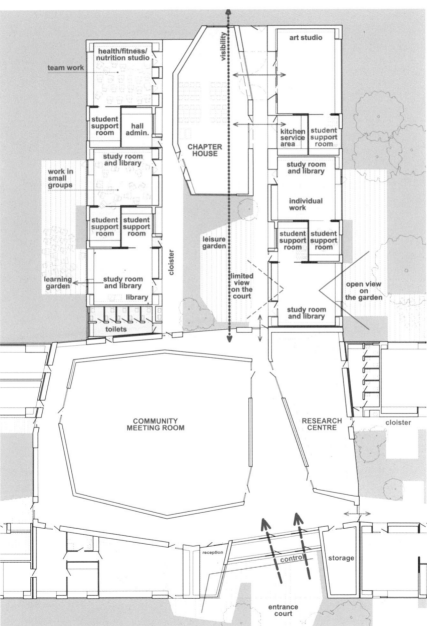

Fig. 9. A detailed plan of the
Foundation Hall

Fig. 10. The Community Meeting Room

facilities. Finally, each Hall has its own Chapter House, which provides the meeting space for the Hall community, as well as being a performance, social and dining space (see Figure 10).

Whilst each Hall is a self-contained 'holding environment', each looks out from itself to its learning gardens as well as into itself to the inner courtyard, and is linked physically and visually to the Community Meeting Room and the Research Centre at the heart of the school.

There is in this design a strong sense of each Hall as a defined learning community, which can organise its weekly programme independently of the other Halls. However, it is also important to stress how the design of the Community Meeting Room, and the existence of the all age advisory groups, who work together each week on the Community Programme day, serve to integrate the whole school community.

Finally, I ask three questions to school leaders, to teachers, to parents, to education policy makers, to business leaders and above all to students:

1. Would this organisation and design have provided a school setting where young people would be significantly challenged and committed to achieve their academic potential?

2. Would this model, which puts relationships at its heart, address the issue of the widening gap between those who currently achieve well in our schools, and the significant and growing underclass of young people who are leaving our schools now, angry and alienated, with few qualifications, unable to secure employment, and with little stake in our society?

3. Would Harry and Kirsten, Devlin and Jackie, and so many students like them, who seem to have been institutionally excluded from our present secondary school offer, have prospered in this model of Urban Village Schooling and have had an experience which they might have been able to look back on with affection and pride?

AFTERWORD
Working with passion and commitment on behalf of young people

In the introduction to this book I quoted Jon Coles, Director General of Schools in England and Wales, in his response to a study finding that in one British city 15 per cent of youngsters aged 16 to 24 not in education, employment or training died within ten years mostly as a result of risky behaviours including drug-taking, binge-drinking and violent crime.

We have to be passionate about the way we educate *all* our children and in particular the disaffected and difficult to engage young. If we are to be successful in this we need to turn this passion into commitments. These commitments are challenging and lie at the heart of the concept of Urban Village Schools as Learning and Research Communities.

There should be a commitment to all our young people that:

- we will offer them an experience of schooling with which they can engage fully and achieve their academic potential;
- they will have the chance to grow up and learn in a community that fosters shared values;
- they will have an experience of schooling on which they can look back with affection;
- their experience of school will ensure that they will have a positive role and stake in our society.

These commitments must be based in a deep sense of care for all young people and in particular for those who express their needs to us in ways which are so often difficult to accept. It is an enormous requirement to ask of our educators. It involves the task of building emotional capital within our school communities; recognising that every conversation, intervention, exchange, every day, every week, needs to leave young people with more self knowledge, self esteem, and understanding about how to live in their school community; the task of creating, designing and organising emotionally supportive settings in which all young people will want to engage and learn.

Achieving this will depend on a predisposition to listen to, reflect on and above all to interpret behaviour. Urban Village Schools will need to demonstrate an understanding that education is about providing a container for the anxieties that so many young people come to school with; an understanding that we need to work with the necessary confusion of adolescence, an approach that respects its processes and speaks to its concerns.

Urban Village Schools: Putting relationships at the heart of school organisation and design is an urgent call for us to set aside preconceived notions and think deeply about what will work best for young people who are currently finding secondary school so difficult.

This book is dedicated to those young people – in the hope that their case will be heard and their needs will be met. We look to politicians and education policy makers to respond to this call – to support us in seeing the first of many Urban Village Schools take shape in our inner city communities.

James Wetz
Bristol 2009

REFERENCES

Introduction

1. M. Tomlinson, 'Thousands drop out of school at 14', *Daily Telegraph* (23 February 2009); R. Cassen and D. Kingdon, *Tackling Low Educational Achievement* (York, Joseph Rowntree Foundation, 2007), p. 66
2. J. Wetz, *Holding Children in Mind over Time* (Bristol, Business West, 2006)
3. J. Bradshaw, P. Hoelscher, D. Richardson, *Child Poverty in Perspective: An overview of child well-being in rich countries* (UNICEF, Florence, Innocenti Research Centre, 2007); R. Layard and J. Dunn, *A Good Childhood: Searching for values in a competitive age* (London, The Children's Society, Penguin, 2009); Cassen and Kingdon (2007), see note 1; Wetz (2006), see note 2
4. Wetz (2006), see note 2
5. Collaborative Center for Education, *Progress and Promise: Results from the Boston Pilot Schools* (Boston, CCE, 2006)
6. L. Clark, 'One in six long-term young jobless "dead within ten years"', *Daily Mail* (7 August 2009)

Chapter One

7. M. Benn and F. Millar, *A Comprehensive Future: Quality and equality for all our children* (London, Compass, 2006), p. 23
8. K. Haines and M. Drakeford, *Young People and Youth Justice* (London, MacMillan, 1999), p. 1
9. B. Goldson, *The New Youth Justice* (Lyme Regis, Russell House, 2000)
10. P. Foley, J. Roche and S. Tucker, eds, *Children in Society: Contemporary theory, policy and practice* (Basingstoke, Palgrave Macmillan, 2001), p. 40
11. Foley, Roche and Tucker, eds (2001), p. 30, see note 10
12. S. Moore, 'British Childhood: Our children need a new deal', *New Statesman* (3 July 2008), p. 26
13. Moore (2008), p. 28, see note 12
14. R. Wingfield, 'Teenage Killings: Loss, trauma and abandonment in the history of young people in trouble', *Attachment* Vol 2 (3), 2008, pp. vii-xii
15. J. Bowlby, *Attachment and Loss* Trilogy (London, Hogarth Press, 1969–80)
16. *The Guardian* (20 December 2008)
17. W. Jordan, *Social Value in Policies for Children: Welfare and well-being,* paper presented to the Centre for Social Policy at Dartington (2008)
18. J. Bowlby, *A Secure Base: Clinical applications of attachment theory* (London, Routledge, 1998)
19. Foley, Roche and Tucker, eds (2001), p. 33, see note 10
20. Jordan (2008), see note 17
21. M. Bunting, 'From buses to blogs, a pathological individualism is poisoning public life', *The Guardian* (28 January 2008)
22. Bradshaw, Hoelscher and Richardson (2007), see note 3
23. BBC News, 'UK is accused of failing children' (14 February 2007)
24. C. Marshall, 'Experts from all disciplines line up to endorse the UN indictment', *The Independent* (14 February 2007)
25. BBC News (2007), see note 23.
26. R. Wilkinson and K. Pickett, *The Spirit Level: Why more equal societies almost always do better* (London, Allen Lane, 2009), pp. 4–5
27. Wilkinson and Pickett (2009), p. 42, see note 26
28. Wilkinson and Pickett (2009), p. 43, see note 26

29. Layard and Dunn (2009), see note 3
30. R. Gilbert *et al*, 'Burden and consequences of child maltreatment in high income countries', *The Lancet* (December 2008)
31. Cassen and Kingdon (2007), see note 1
32. P. Thomson and L. Russell, *Mapping the Alternatives to Permanent Exclusion* (York, Rowntree, 2007)
33. '344 School Children a Day Suspended for Violence', *The Independent* (1 November 2008)
34. Home Office, *Youth Crime Action Plan* (London, COI, 2008)
35. S. Parke, *Children and Young People in Custody: An analysis of the experience of 15–18 year olds in prison* (London, HM Inspectorate of Prisons and Youth Justice Board, 2009)
36. *Bromley Briefings Prison Factfile June 2009* (London, Prison Reform Trust, 2009)
37. J. Wetz, 'The Children Left Behind', *Dispatches* (London, Channel 4, 11 February 2008)
38. Wetz (2006), p. 1, see note 2
39. A. Hill, 'Depressed, Stressed: Teachers in Crisis', *The Observer* (31 August 2008)
40. Department for Education and Skills, *Building Schools for the Future: Consultation on a new approach to capital investment* (London, DfES, 2003), p. 3

Chapter Two
41. L. Raphael Reed, C. Croudace, N. Harrison, A. Baxter and K. Last, *Young Participation in Higher Education: A sociocultural study of educational engagement in Bristol South Parliamentary Constituency* (Bristol, The University of the West of England and the Higher Education Funding Council for England, 2007), p. 174
42. Wetz (2006), see note 2

Chapter Three
43. D. Meier, *The Power of Their Ideas: Lessons for America from a small school in Harlem* (Boston, Beacon Press,1995), p. 118
44. T. Vander Ark in Foreword to T. Toch, *High Schools on a Human Scale: How small schools can transform American education* (Boston, Beacon Press, 2003), p. ix–x
45. E.L. Boyer, *High School: A report on secondary education in America* (New York, Harper & Row, 1983); T. Sizer, *Horace's Compromise: The dilemma of the American high school* (Boston, Mariner Books, 1984)
46. Wetz (2007), see note 37
47. Meier (1995), p. 113, see note 43
48. L. Raphael Reed, *Occasional notes as commentary for Urban Village School report* (2008)
49. See www.dcsf.gov.uk/everychildmatters/about/
50. R. Tung and M. Ouimette, *Strong Results, High Demand: A four-year study of Boston's Pilot High Schools* (Boston, Center for Collaborative Education, 2007), p. v
51. M. Osborn, 'National Context, Educational Goals and Pupil Experience of Schooling and Learning in Three European Countries', *Compare*, Volume 29, Number 3 (1999), pp. 287–301
52. P. Bennett, 'From secondary school blues to lifelong learning? Aspects of the retrospective reevaluation of formative educational experience by adults', *International Journal of Lifelong Education*, Volume 18, Number 3 (1999), pp. 155–174
53. European Commission, *European Report on the Quality of School Education: Sixteen quality indicators* (Luxembourg, Office for Official Publications of the European Communities, 2001), p. 34

Chapter Four
54. A. Aynsley-Green, 'Treat Children with Respect and You'll Get It Straight Back', *The Guardian* (19 January 2006)
55. H. Geddes, *Attachment in the Classroom: The links between children's early experience, emotional well-being and performance in school* (UK, Worth Publishing, 2006), p. 142
56. B. Youell, *The Learning Relationship: Psychoanalytic thinking in education* (London, Karnac Books, 2006), p. 7

57. Youell (2006), p. 3, see note 56
58. Youell (2006), p. 24, see note 56
59. D.W. Winnicott, *The Maturational Processes and the Facilitating Environment* (London, Karnac, 1965)
60. L.A. Sroufe, 'Infant-caregiver Attachment Patterns of Adaptation in Preschool: The roots of maladaptation and competence' in *Minnesota Symposia of Child Psychology* Vol. 16, ed. M. Perlmutter (Hillsdale, New Jersey, Lawrence Erlbaum, 1983), p. 61
61. D. Howe, *Attachment Theory for Social Work Practice* (Basingstoke, Palgrave, 1995)
62. Youell (2006), p. 82, see note 56
63. A. Ward, K. Kasinski, J. Pooley and A. Worthington, *Therapeutic Communities for Children and Young People* (London, Jessica Kingsley, 2003), p. 168
64. Ward *et al*, (2003), p. 168, see note 63
65. Ward *et al*, (2003), p. 119, see note 63
66. I. Menzies Lyth, *Containing Anxiety in Institutions: Selected essays* (London, Free Association Books, 1988)
67. E.H. Erikson, *Childhood and Society* (New York, W.W. Norton, 1963)
68. E. Miller, *From Dependence to Autonomy: Studies in organisation and change* (London, Free Association Books, 1993); Menzies Lyth (1988), see note 66
69. Ward *et al*, (2003), p. 167, see note 63

Chapter Five
70. C. Leadbeater, 'A Neet solution', *New Statesman* (10 July 2008) p. 16
71. G. Bénédicte, 'Le capital émotionnel et genre: Ce capital qui fait aussi la différence entre les filles et les garçons à l'école et au travail', *Les Cahiers de la Maison des Sciences Economiques, série rouge,* no. 76 (Paris, Université Panthéon-Sorbonne, Centre d'Economie de la Sorbonne & CEREQ, 2006), p. 26
72. K.L. Wahlstrom, 'The Prickly Politics of School Starting Times', *Phi, Delta, Kappan,* Volume 80, Number 5 (1999), pp. 344–7
73 T. Wagner, *Making the Grade: Re-Inventing the American High School* (New York, Routledge Falmer, 2003)
74. See www.thersa.org/projects/education/opening-minds
75. See www.edisonschools.com/edison-schools/school-design-curriculum/curriculum
76. See www.futurelab.org.uk/projects/enquiring-minds; www.bostonartsacademy.org/pages/baa_about/mission_vision; www.fenwayhs.org/cityclass
77. P. Bourdieu, 'The Forms of Capital', English version published in J.G. Richardson, *Handbook of Theory and Research for the Sociology of Education* (New Hampshire, Greenwood, 1986), pp. 241–258
78. L. Raphael Reed (2008), see note 48

Chapter Six
79. Wetz (2007), see note 37
80. See W. Wallace, *Schools within Schools: Human scale education in practice* (London, Calouste Gulbenkian Foundation, 2009)
81. Wetz (2007), see note 37

James Wetz is Visiting Fellow at the University of Bristol Graduate School of Education, and worked for over 30 years in state secondary education, 16 of these as a headteacher. He is a Fellow of the RSA and of the Centre for Social Policy at the Warren House Group in Dartington. He published the report *Holding Children in Mind over Time* (2006) and researched and presented the documentary 'The Children Left Behind' for Channel 4's *Dispatches* series in 2008.